Oliver Mattausch

Visibility Algorithms for Real-Time Rendering

Oliver Mattausch

Visibility Algorithms for Real-Time Rendering

Efficient Visibility Computations for Rendering Acceleration and High-Quality Illumination in General 3D Environments

Südwestdeutscher Verlag für Hochschulschriften

Impressum/Imprint (nur für Deutschland/ only for Germany)
Bibliografische Information der Deutschen Nationalbibliothek: Die Deutsche Nationalbibliothek verzeichnet diese Publikation in der Deutschen Nationalbibliografie; detaillierte bibliografische Daten sind im Internet über http://dnb.d-nb.de abrufbar.

Alle in diesem Buch genannten Marken und Produktnamen unterliegen warenzeichen-, marken- oder patentrechtlichem Schutz bzw. sind Warenzeichen oder eingetragene Warenzeichen der jeweiligen Inhaber. Die Wiedergabe von Marken, Produktnamen, Gebrauchsnamen, Handelsnamen, Warenbezeichnungen u.s.w. in diesem Werk berechtigt auch ohne besondere Kennzeichnung nicht zu der Annahme, dass solche Namen im Sinne der Warenzeichen- und Markenschutzgesetzgebung als frei zu betrachten wären und daher von jedermann benutzt werden dürften.

Verlag: Südwestdeutscher Verlag für Hochschulschriften GmbH & Co. KG
Dudweiler Landstr. 99, 66123 Saarbrücken, Deutschland
Telefon +49 681 37 20 271-1, Telefax +49 681 37 20 271-0
Email: info@svh-verlag.de
Zugl.: Wien, TU, Diss., 2010

Herstellung in Deutschland:
Schaltungsdienst Lange o.H.G., Berlin
Books on Demand GmbH, Norderstedt
Reha GmbH, Saarbrücken
Amazon Distribution GmbH, Leipzig
ISBN: 978-3-8381-1887-1

Imprint (only for USA, GB)
Bibliographic information published by the Deutsche Nationalbibliothek: The Deutsche Nationalbibliothek lists this publication in the Deutsche Nationalbibliografie; detailed bibliographic data are available in the Internet at http://dnb.d-nb.de.

Any brand names and product names mentioned in this book are subject to trademark, brand or patent protection and are trademarks or registered trademarks of their respective holders. The use of brand names, product names, common names, trade names, product descriptions etc. even without a particular marking in this works is in no way to be construed to mean that such names may be regarded as unrestricted in respect of trademark and brand protection legislation and could thus be used by anyone.

Publisher: Südwestdeutscher Verlag für Hochschulschriften GmbH & Co. KG
Dudweiler Landstr. 99, 66123 Saarbrücken, Germany
Phone +49 681 37 20 271-1, Fax +49 681 37 20 271-0
Email: info@svh-verlag.de

Printed in the U.S.A.
Printed in the U.K. by (see last page)
ISBN: 978-3-8381-1887-1

Copyright © 2010 by the author and Südwestdeutscher Verlag für Hochschulschriften GmbH & Co. KG and licensors
All rights reserved. Saarbrücken 2010

I would like to thank Jiri Bittner for a long and fruitful scientific relationship, who acted both as a guidance as well as scientific collaborator during the time of my thesis. I also want to thank my advicer Michael Wimmer for his ability to motivate, and his sharp analysis and criticism of my work. Most of all I would like to express my gratitude to parents for their support. Without these people this work would not have been possible. Last but not least I want to thank my co-workers of the rendering research group in Vienna for a good work environment and valuable discussions.

Oliver Mattausch

Vienna, 1.10.2010

Contents

1	**Introduction**		**1**
	1.1	Motivation	1
	1.2	Visibility culling	3
		1.2.1 Definition	3
		1.2.2 Problem relevance	5
		1.2.3 Other applications	6
		1.2.4 Visibility preprocessing versus online culling	7
		1.2.5 Rasterization versus raytracing	9
	1.3	Quantitative visibility for realistic lighting	10
		1.3.1 The rendering equation	10
		1.3.2 Ambient occlusion	11
	1.4	Main contributions	12
	1.5	Structure of this thesis	14
2	**Related Work**		**15**
	2.1	Techniques for real-time rendering	15
		2.1.1 Render-time estimation and calibration	17
	2.2	Hierarchical subdivision schemes	18
		2.2.1 Space subdivisions versus object hierarchies	19
		2.2.2 Bounding volume hierarchy	20
		2.2.3 Binary space partitioning	22
		2.2.4 kD-tree	22
		2.2.5 Octree	22
		2.2.6 Grid and hierarchical grid	24
		2.2.7 Surface area heuristics	24
	2.3	Methods for rendering simplification	25
		2.3.1 Level of detail	25
		2.3.2 Image-based rendering	26
	2.4	Visibility culling	29
		2.4.1 Methods for scene preprocessing	29
		2.4.2 Visibility preprocessing	35

	2.4.3	Online occlusion culling	46
	2.4.4	Hybrid rendering systems	52
2.5	Visibility computations for realistic lighting		55
	2.5.1	Shadow algorithms	56
	2.5.2	Real-time global illumination	57
	2.5.3	Ambient occlusion	64
2.6	Reprojection techniques for temporal coherence		74

3 Algorithms for Scene Preprocessing   79

3.1	Introduction		79
3.2	Global visibility sampling		81
	3.2.1	Sample distributions	83
3.3	Problem definition		84
	3.3.1	Render cost model	85
3.4	Adaptive visibility-driven view cell construction		86
	3.4.1	What is a good view cell partition?	86
	3.4.2	Overview	88
	3.4.3	Adaptive view cell construction	90
	3.4.4	Using the view cell hierarchy	94
	3.4.5	Results	95
	3.4.6	Discussion	104
3.5	Optimized subdivisions for preprocessed visibility		105
	3.5.1	Outline	107
	3.5.2	Framework for interleaved subdivisions	108
	3.5.3	Optimization approach	109
	3.5.4	Visibility sampling	112
	3.5.5	Subdivision	114
	3.5.6	Results	118
3.6	Conclusions		122

4 CHC++: Coherent Hierarchical Culling Revisited   125

4.1	Introduction	125
4.2	Overview	128

	4.2.1	CHC and its problems 128
	4.2.2	NOHC and its problems 129
4.3	Our algorithm 130	
	4.3.1	Building blocks of CHC++ 130
	4.3.2	Reducing state changes 131
	4.3.3	Reducing the number of queries 134
	4.3.4	Tight bounding volumes 139
	4.3.5	Previously frustum-culled nodes 141
	4.3.6	Putting it all together 144
4.4	Results 146	
4.5	Conclusions 150	

5 High Quality Screen-Space Ambient Occlusion using Temporal Coherence   153

5.1	Introduction 154	
5.2	Our algorithm 156	
	5.2.1	SSAO generation 156
	5.2.2	Reprojection 157
	5.2.3	Temporal refinement 158
	5.2.4	Detecting and dealing with invalid pixels 160
	5.2.5	Dealing with undersampled regions 163
	5.2.6	Optimizations 165
5.3	Results 166	
5.4	Conclusion 171	

6 Conclusions and Future Work   173

6.1	Synopsis 173	
6.2	Analysis of the proposed algorithms 175	
	6.2.1	Combining our algorithms 176
6.3	Future work 177	
	6.3.1	Striving for simplicity 178
	6.3.2	A combined algorithm using PVSs and hardware occlusion queries 178

	6.3.3	Reverse visibility for interactive scene editing 179
	6.3.4	Optimal hierarchy construction for online culling . . . 179
	6.3.5	Robust and efficient exact visibility 180
	6.3.6	Real-time global illumination 180
	6.3.7	Reprojection and temporal coherence 181
6.4	Conclusions 181

*The true mystery of the world is
the visible, not the invisible.*

Oscar Wilde

1

Introduction

The topic of this thesis are algorithms for visibility computations, both as a preprocess and online, that are general and useable in any type of 3D environment, and enable us to achieve real-time frame rates with the best possible image quality. The most intuitive and well-known application of visibility computations is the removal of geometry hidden from a view point in order to accelerate rendering. This is the main focus of this thesis, but we will also investigate quantitative visibility computations for high-quality shading, with a focus on the popular ambient occlusion method. Our algorithms are designed for standard consumer graphics hardware using APIs like OpenGL or Direct3D.

In this chapter we will first give an outline of our problem domain and some basic definitions. We discuss the motivations behind our research on visibility problems, and the applications and relevance of visibility computations for the acceleration of real-time rendering and for realistic illumination. At last we state the main contributions of this thesis.

1.1 Motivation

Real-time rendering is the art of rendering graphics in the best possible quality within 60 frames per second. Real-time rendering is essential for interactive applications – anything less can lead to side effects like dropped frames or delayed control, which seriously disturb the perceived sensation. Over the

Chapter 1. Introduction

Figure 1.1: Evolution of the model complexity over a period of only a few years: The Vienna model (1M triangles), the Powerplant (12M triangles), and the Boeing model (350M triangles).

years real-time graphics has evolved tremendously – thanks to better graphics hardware, more detailed models, and better techniques, while the challenges to researchers and developers become more and more sophisticated. Modern high-profile games stun their audience with better and better image quality in real time, and there is a fierce competition over who has has the better rendering algorithms, which gives them the leading edge. In order to provide the best image quality, game developers use a long time to fine-tune every aspect of their games. However there is also another side to real-time rendering, for example the interactive visualization of large datasets that e.g., come from satellite images. In this case, the challenge is to create tools that can automate all the steps required to render such complex scenes in real time. Hence it is very important to create powerful algorithms for real-time acceleration and realistic real-time illumination. In this thesis, we focus on the different forms of *visibility computations*, which are an essential part of most real-time rendering methods.

Visibility computations belong to the most fundamental operations in computer graphics. They are inherently difficult to handle, as they are of global nature, and it is impossible to provide an analytic solution for scenes with complex visibility interactions. In this thesis we want to show that it is possible to achieve *output-sensitive* high-quality rendering in real time for any scene configuration by solving the visibility computations efficiently. Output sensitivity is the beneficial property of an algorithm that the rendering time depends only on the output. In terms of computer graphics, the rendering time must not be driven by the actual scene complexity (consider brute force rasterization that always renders the whole scene), but only by the complexity of the objects that are actually visible. Ideally, no computational resources should be wasted on things that do not contribute to the final image.

In order to reach our goals, we have to investigate and optimize both *qualitative* and *quantitative* visibility computations. Qualitative visibility (what is visible?) corresponds to problems like binary visibility culling and hard shadows. Qualitative visibility (how much is visible?), on the other hand, corresponds to problems like soft shadows or ambient occlusion. These are rather expensive techniques to compute in real-time, but at the same time absolutely important ingredients for making images look realistic. We think that it is necessary to develop intelligent yet stable solutions to these problems that are usable in practical applications with standard consumer hardware.

Another recurring theme in this thesis is *temporal* and *spatial coherence*. In real-time rendering, a new image is generated every fraction of a second, hence the difference between two consecutive frames is only minimal in most cases, as the view point will be almost the same, and the pose and position of animated characters will only change slightly. We want to show that spatial and temporal coherence can be exploited in several ways to improve and accelerate rendering algorithms.

1.2 Visibility culling

1.2.1 Definition

The task of discarding primitives as fast as possible, in order to draw only those that are visible from the current view point, is called *visibility culling*. The main use of visibility culling is rendering acceleration by reducing overdraw and reaching output sensitivity (see Figure 1.2). While visibility classifications are inherently solved for ray tracing, it is a difficult problem for the overwhelmingly predominant group of renderers based on rasterization, as provided by consumer graphics cards.

Chapter 1. Introduction

Figure 1.2: (left) Using visibility culling, we send only the visible buildings bordering to the street (shown as red roofs in the small overview window) to the graphics card for a low view point. (right) This is only a fraction of the buildings rendered for a high view point.

There are several classifications for visibility problems [COCSD02, BW03]. The two problems that got the most attention are 1) visibility from a region, which corresponds to preprocessed visibility, and 2) visibility from a point, which corresponds to online visibility culling. In preprocessed visibility, we aim to find the *Potentially Visible Set* (PVS) for a set of view cells. Preprocessing has the advantage that once the PVS is found, it requires practically no additional overhead during rendering, and support for PVS-based rendering is easily integrated into any rendering engine. On the contrary, online occlusion culling requires no preprocessing and works also for dynamic environments.

Another classification separates visibility algorithms into *aggressive* and *conservative* methods, which corresponds to underestimation and overestimation of the PVS, respectively. If there is no over- or underestimation, we speak of exact solutions, if there potentially is both over- and underestimation, the solution is approximate. In practice, exact solution are of little practical relevance, because they are both slow and prune to numerical errors. Sampling-based methods are inherently aggressive in their nature, but they are more stable, and experiments indicate that in practice they may be more accurate than theoretically exact algorithms [WWZ*06].

1.2. Visibility culling

1.2.2 Problem relevance

We feel that despite many years of working on algorithms for visibility culling, some basic research problems have not been sufficiently solved, which prevents a wide-spread use of intelligent and efficient tools for visibility, and we want to contribute to close this gap. In the following we discuss why new visibility research in various areas is still important nowadays.

Some people argue that the growing power of modern graphics hardware makes visibility culling obsolete. Actually the opposite is true – even with the newest graphics hardware, good visibility culling is a requirement for many applications. Faster graphics hardware goes along with more complex models and shaders. This fact is illustrated in Figure 1.1. Visualizing a city model like Vienna with 1M triangles was considered an immensely challenging task some years ago. Models like the Powerplant with 12M triangles are still challenging today to render in full resolution, but they are simple compared to the Boeing model which has nearly *30 times* more triangles. For example, rendering the inner parts like the accurately modeled cockpit while only the outside of the plane is visible would be a huge waste and an overkill for any consumer hardware.

Good visibility culling is especially crucial in game development. In order to satisfy the need for spectacular state-of-the-art graphics, game programmers cannot afford wasting processing time on hidden geometry, which could otherwise be spent on more realistic shaders. In game development, a significant share of project man-months goes into calculating and optimizing the visibility in a scene. Recently, there is a rapid evolution of applications like *Google Earth*, which require processing immense amounts of data in an interactive or dynamic fashion. Rendering such large amounts of data in a naive way is virtually impossible. A real-time visualization in acceptable quality raises some interesting issues for the research community to solve, and also adds new requirements to the used visibility algorithms in terms of flexibility and scalability. Other examples for extremely complex scenes are large vegetation scenes like forests. Many trees will be visible only through small holes, nevertheless they will be rendered despite contributing almost

Chapter 1. Introduction

nothing to the final image. Such massive scenes often cannot be handled by visibility alone – a combination of visibility with other techniques like image-based rendering or polygonal level of detail is required to achieve acceptable frame rates.

1.2.3 Other applications

Visibility culling has important applications in a variety of fields besides computer graphics and rendering. There are several applications in computer vision, for example the task of optimal sensor placing for surveillance [AAT93, LMD05] (solving the well-known art gallery problem), motion planning for robotics [NSL99, MCTH05]), or computational geometry. Many visibility culling methods used for rendering acceleration will be applicable for tasks within other fields with little or no modifications. A topic that became very popular recently is using visibility culling for sound propagation [LSLS09, CATM09], where visibility has to be computed efficiently for hundreds of potential receiver points.

Another example is the case of *line-of-sight* (LOS) algorithms. Line-of-sight algorithms are used to find the mutual visibility between objects – this problem basically corresponds to a of from-region visibility problem. For example, line-of-sight computations are required in computer games (e.g., we evaluate if an enemy can see the player from a certain region), where errors can lead to unwanted changes in the game play. Mutual visibility must also be queried in online multiplayer games that use peer-to-peer communication, in order to find out if communication must be established between a pair of players. Evidently, fast line-of-sight algorithms are of great importance in simulations that require some kind of real-time response, such as simulations for disaster control, emergency management, or military scenarios. There can be thousands of independent units which can potentially see each other, hence millions of mutual visibility relations must be evaluated in a fraction of a second. Solving these relations uses up a huge share of the processing time of the simulation, which could be otherwise used for something else, e.g., better artificial intelligence. Some approaches to solve this highly parallelizable problem involve multiple units of GPUs [SGS*04, VMH*05].

1.2.4 Visibility preprocessing versus online culling

In the scope of this thesis we investigate both visibility preprocessing and online culling. In this section we discuss the reasons why we chose to work on both paradigms, compare their applications and their individual strengths.

Visibility preprocessing Visibility preprocessing has been studied since the early nineties [Tel92b]. The mechanism creates practically no overhead, and can be easily integrated into any engine on demand. During walkthrough, we just have to locate the current view cell, and render all the objects in its PVS. On the downside, it is inherently difficult for visibility preprocessing to handle dynamic scenes. Simple and powerful visibility preprocessing algorithms (or visibility "solvers") exist for special scenarios like indoor or city scenes [LG95a]. However, handling general 3D scenes with preprocessing is a tough problem, and most proposed solutions are either prone to robustness issues, slow, or aggressive in nature, meaning that they are likely to suffer from visibility errors. Until recently there were virtually no solvers on the market that provide satisfactory results in terms of robustness and speed for general scenarios like outdoor scenes, or even worse for difficult scenarios like massive foliage scenes.

While many solutions have been proposed for computing preprocessed visibility, only a very small number of papers deal with optimizing the *input* to the preprocessed visibility algorithm, i.e., creating the view cells and the objects, which are usually assumed to be given. Partitioning of the scene into view cells and objects is a process that scene designers usually do by hand. Having a tool that automatically creates a good set of view cells or set of objects in terms of rendering efficiency and memory cost would make this time-consuming task obsolete. Obviously, just making the view cells so small that they are almost singular view points, or solving the visibility on a triangle level is not feasible, because the memory cost for managing the PVSs would explode. Going one step further, in order to create subdivisions

Chapter 1. Introduction

which are optimal for rendering, view space and object space subdivisions cannot be treated separately. Instead, we have to investigate the *combined* optimization of both view space and object space subdivisions.

Online occlusion culling Since occlusion queries [BMH98] have become supported by graphics hardware, the direction of research has shifted from preprocessed visibility towards online occlusion culling. Most online culling algorithms are naturally image based – we only have to draw objects which contribute to the rendered image in the current frame. In theory online culling is very appealing for developers because it requires no preprocessing, can handle arbitrary scenes, and allows algorithms that are conceptually quite simple and easy to implement. In particular it naturally allows the handling of dynamic scenes, which is inherently difficult to do with preprocessing. Despite their huge potential, online occlusion culling algorithms have been rarely used in actual engines or games, at best they were integrated as an alternative to rendering methods using plain view-frustum culling for some good reasons – from our practical experience with popular engines like Ogre3D we know that there are cases where a simple algorithm performing only view-frustum culling is faster than sophisticated occlusion culling algorithms. Most existing online culling algorithm are notoriously hardware unfriendly, and do not integrate well into existing engine designs. One goal of this thesis is to develop strategies to avoid these disadvantages.

Discussion Considering the apparent advantages of online occlusion culling, the question may arise whether we still need preprocessing once an efficient online occlusion culling algorithm has been found. Our answer would be a clear yes. We believe that both visibility preprocessing and online occlusion culling have important applications, as well as a lot of potential for improvements. Both approaches have their strengths and weaknesses, hence we want to investigate both of them. For example, algorithms for visibility preprocessing have the reputation of being notoriously difficult to implement. On the other hand, the visibility solver itself is independent from the engine and can be shipped in the form of a stand-alone program. It requires only little

1.2. Visibility culling

change to an existing engine to include the resulting visibility solution in the form of view cells and their corresponding PVSs, while the inner rendering loop remains untouched. On the other hand, hardware-based occlusion culling algorithms can be challenging to implement into modern engines, as they require changes to the innermost rendering loop. Also, as long as there is enough memory to keep the PVSs, using preprocessed visibility is guaranteed to impose very little runtime overhead on any configuration of hard- and software. We also have to keep in mind that visibility preprocessing has a wide range of applications other than pure rendering, some of which we mentioned before.

1.2.5 Rasterization versus raytracing

Some people believe that rasterization as performed by modern GPUs will be obsolete in a couple of years and will be replaced by real-time ray tracing [RSH05], and therefore there will also be no use for visibility culling. The arguments are that ray tracing scales better with the scene complexity, and that ray tracing produces more realistic images because it can be used to do reflections and refractions, and will make global illumination feasible in the future.

We think that this transition is unlikely to happen in the near future. First of all, the argument about better scalability is true only if compared to naive brute-force rasterization. Ray tracing has such a good runtime behavior of $O(\log n)$ in the number of primitives because it creates a *scene hierarchy* that immensely accelerates the spatial search for the next intersection point. Also, ray tracing has natural output sensitive behavior because it is image based, and less rays are required for small distant objects. One has to realize that it is possible to achieve the same beneficial runtime behavior in rasterization with hierarchical visibility culling combined with level-of-detail or image-based rendering.

On the other hand, ray tracing has several disadvantages: An efficient ray tracing implementation is highly dependent on hardware specific optimizations. Likewise, ray tracing is not as straightforward to parallelize as

Chapter 1. Introduction

it seems – the hierarchical structures are inherently difficult to implement robustly and to traverse fast on parallel hardware. Also, ray tracing has the inherent problem of casting infinitely thin rays at a time, which can lead to aliasing. Furthermore, ray tracing can be optimized mainly for coherent primary rays. Secondary rays from reflections and refractions are less coherent and hence have less potential to be optimized. Rasterization achieves similar effects very efficiently with techniques like environment maps and shadow maps. Accurate global illumination in real time is still impossible with either technique.

1.3 Quantitative visibility for realistic lighting

1.3.1 The rendering equation

Visibility computations are of immense importance for any field of computer graphics that aims to solve the rendering equation [Kaj86, ATS94], which computes the radiance emitted into direction ω from point p:

$$L(p,\omega) = L_e(p,\omega) + \frac{1}{\pi}\int_\Omega f_r(p,\omega',\omega)L_i(p,\omega')(\omega \cdot n)d\omega'. \quad (1.1)$$

L_e is the self emission, f_r is the *bidirectional reflectance distribution function* (BRDF), L_i is the incident light from direction ω', and n is the surface normal. Its evaluation requires solving complex visibility interactions, which eventually become the bottleneck of most algorithms that compute realistic lighting effects, like shadows, global illumination, or ambient occlusion. These problems have a one-to-one correspondence with problems from visibility culling. For example, hard and soft shadows correspond to from-point and from-region visibility, respectively. View cells are often treated as area light sources in literature, where invisible objects correspond to those that lie in the *umbra* region of a view cell, while objects that lie in the *penumbra* are visible from one or more view points, but not from all of them. Visibility

1.3. Quantitative visibility for realistic lighting

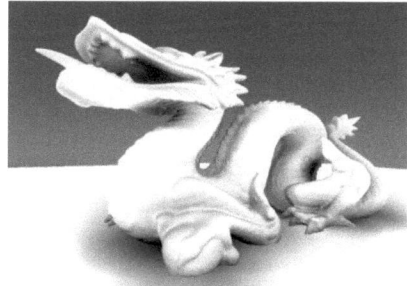

Figure 1.3: Buddha and Dragon models rendered with ambient occlusion.

queries can be efficiently solved on the hardware by using one or multiple shadow maps [Wil78] to calculate the direct influence of a point or area light source. Shadow maps can be seen as a discretization of the visibility from a light source sample and are thus well suited to be computed with rasterization hardware. Some methods use a gathering or splatting approach to distribute either illumination or shadowing.

1.3.2 Ambient occlusion

One chapter of this thesis deals with ambient occlusion computation. Ambient occlusion is a shading technique that essentially strips down the rendering equation to pure visibility calculations in the hemisphere of a surface point. It evaluates the percentage of the hemisphere which is occluded, assuming a perfectly diffuse material and omitting all further light bounces. Ambient occlusion of a surface point p with normal n is computed as [CT81]

$$\mathrm{AO}(p) = \frac{1}{\pi} \int_\Omega V(p, \omega')(n \cdot \omega') d\omega'. \qquad (1.2)$$

Ω denotes all directions on the hemisphere, and V is the (inverse) binary visibility function, which usually considers obstacles within a certain sampling radius only:

Chapter 1. Introduction

$$V(p,\omega') = \begin{cases} 0 & \text{if direction } \omega' \text{ is blocked} \\ 1, & \text{otherwise.} \end{cases} \quad (1.3)$$

This relatively cheap method gives a great impression of indirect lighting and soft contact shadows, as can be seen in Figure 1.3. Our main interest was to improve screen-space ambient occlusion, a popular variant which uses the depth buffer as discrete scene representation. Screen-space ambient occlusion decouples shading from the scene complexity, which is very important to reach one of our goals – to achieve output sensitivity.

1.4 Main contributions

The contributions of this thesis consist of four peer reviewed conference and journal papers [MBW06, MBWW07, MBW08, MSW10]. We shortly describe our main results.

The first paper describes an algorithm for adaptive view cell construction based on coarse visibility sampling. The algorithm consists of a spatial BSP subdivision of the scene and a subsequent merging step, which are guided by a novel render cost heuristics. A huge body of papers deals with computing the actual visibility in the scene, whereas the important task of automatically computing view cells that are optimized for rendering has been almost neglected before. This is one of only a handful of papers that are dedicated to the problem of view cell construction in particular. The work has been published in Rendering Techniques 2006 (Proceedings of Eurographics Symposium on Rendering), 195-206, June 2006, Nicosia, Cyprus.

The second paper proposes an extension of the previous work on optimized view cell construction, and also utilizes coarsely sampled visibility to guide the subdivision process. Due to their related content, we discuss these methods together in this thesis. The new algorithm constructs interleaved subdivisions of both view space and object space in a way that the *combined subdivisions* are optimized for rendering. The globally progressive subdivision process allows balancing between memory cost and render cost of the

1.4. Main contributions

PVSs. The work has been published in the Proceedings of Graphics Interface 2007, 335-342, May 2007, Montreal, Canada.

The third paper describes an algorithm for efficient online occlusion culling using hardware occlusion queries. The algorithm significantly improves on previous techniques by reducing the overhead induced by the hardware occlusion queries to a minimum, and by making better use of temporal and spatial coherence of visibility. As a result of the new optimizations the number of issued occlusion queries and the number of rendering state changes are significantly reduced. Also, the new algorithm integrates much better with existing game engines, and unlike many previous hierarchical culling algorithms allows efficient material sorting. This work has been published in Computer Graphics Forum (Proceedings of Eurographics), 27(2), 221-230, May 2008.

The fourth paper proposes a high-quality screen-space ambient occlusion algorithm utilizing temporal coherence to accumulate samples over time. We introduce a new invalidation scheme for discovering invalid pixels (i.e., pixels where the assumption of temporal coherence does not hold). Techniques like adaptive sampling and adaptive convergence-aware filtering make this algorithm well suited for fully dynamic scenes. The work has been accepted to appear in Computer Graphics Forum.

Also, the author of this thesis co-authored a paper about a progressive sampling-based algorithm for preprocessed visibility called Adaptive Global Visibility Sampling [BMW*09], which was presented at Siggraph 2009. The algorithm uses some concepts proposed in Chapter 3 about scene preprocessing, and in a way complements this work. Furthermore, he participated in a paper about temporal coherence for soft shadow rendering, which was presented at ISVC 2009 [SSMW09]. This algorithm is related to the work about high-quality ambient occlusion using temporal coherence presented in Chapter 5.

Chapter 1. Introduction

1.5 Structure of this thesis

Chapter 2 investigates the related work in real-time rendering, focusing on visibility computations in particular. Next we describe our four novel algorithms. Both algorithms that deal with optimized scene preprocessing are discussed together in Chapter 3, first the algorithm for view cell generation, then its extension into a combined optimization of view space and object space subdivisions. In Chapter 4 we describe an optimized algorithm for online occlusion culling. In Chapter 5 we propose a screen-space ambient occlusion algorithm that uses temporal coherence and reprojection. At last we give our conclusions and discuss possible future directions in Chapter 6.

What delights us in visible beauty is the invisible.

Marie Von Ebner-Eschenbach

2

Related Work

In this chapter we first discuss the basics requirements of real-time rendering, then we describe techniques for hierarchical subdivision of a 3D scene, which are an integral part of all of our visibility culling algorithms. Next we investigate methods for rendering acceleration: simplification methods using level-of-detail or image-based rendering, and most importantly the main topic of this thesis - visibility culling. At last we discuss the applications of non-binary visibility for realistic lighting, and in particular ambient occlusion algorithms.

2.1 Techniques for real-time rendering

The goal of real-time rendering is to provide the best possible visual quality within at least 60 FPS [Wim01]. For more complex models like the one shown in Figure 2.1, this task requires a number of non-trivial techniques. In practice, we need to also take additional computationally intensive tasks like physics, artificial intelligence, and simulations into account, all of which occupy a share of the available resources. Hence we want to keep the time spent on the actual image synthesis as short possible. In particular we want to avoid wasting processing time on processing geometry that does not contribute to the final image – this is the purpose of visibility culling. Another difficult task for developers of real-time graphics is to balance the load between different processing units on a particular hardware, using all processing

Chapter 2. Related Work

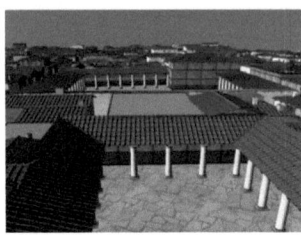

Figure 2.1: The goal of real-time rendering is to render views like this in the complex Pompeii model (40M triangles) with more than 30 FPS.

units to their full capacity. In the case of standard PC hardware, this usually involves the synchronization of a multicore CPU and one or two graphics processing units (GPU), but the trend goes to more and more parallizable hardware. Programming APIs like CUDA or OpenCL allow massively parallel programming, and in case of high-end consoles like the Playstation 3, a couple of cell processor units must be synchronized.

Trivial acceleration techniques that are part of virtually any real time application are *backface culling*, where backfacing polygons are pruned early, and *view-frustum culling*, where a simple bounding geometry of an object is tested for intersection with the view frustum. Only if the bounding geometry intersects the view frustum, the object itself is potentially visible and has to be rendered. Like many other techniques, view-frustum culling scales much better with the scene complexity when used in a hierarchical fashion [AM00], reducing the complexity from $O(n)$ to $O(\log(n))$ in the number of objects.

To determine the visible objects early and achieve output sensitivity, we require visibility culling. However, visibility culling as a stand-alone technique can generally not guarantee a sufficient frame rate. Hence visibility culling is often used in combination with simplification techniques like *level-of-detail* or *image-based rendering*.

Game studios invest a huge amount of time and effort into careful level design and subsequent play testing to guarantee real-time frame rates and to avoid *visibility hotspots* (i.e., view points where too much is visible, causing frame rate drops) [ED07]. Unfortunately, such a fine tuning of a scene is not

2.1. Techniques for real-time rendering

possible if data and hardware is not known in advance, and some applications rely on more automatized methods.

2.1.1 Render-time estimation and calibration

Automatic acceleration and load-balancing techniques aim to provide the best possible image quality with constraints on the required frame rate. Funkhouser and Sequin. [FS93] proposed a predictive load-balancing system that solves a variant of the *knapsack problem*, where the items are different level-of-details, and the weights are their predicted rendering times. The system bounds the frame time by choosing the appropriate level-of-detail based on a rendering time estimation. They use the following cost-benefit heuristics:

$$RT(x) = \max(C_p|p(x)|, C_v|v(x)|, C_f|f(x)|), \tag{2.1}$$

where $|p(x)|$, $|v(x)|$, $|f(x)|$ are the number of polygons, vertices, and fragments, respectively, and C is the associated cost. It is crucial for any load balancing system to use a formula that reliably estimates the rendering time. Unfortunately, this particular formula is targeted to older systems and not usable without modifications on new hardware with modern GPUs.

An alternative to such predictive system are reactive systems [RH94] that correct their workload based on the actual frame time. However, these systems cannot guarantee a bounded frame time, and they have to be carefully tuned to be sufficiently responsive for reacting to swift changes on the one hand, and to avoid hysteresis effects on the other hand.

Wimmer and Wonka [WW03] proposed a rendering time estimation that is more fitted to the demands of newer hardware, and the use of dedicated GPUs in particular. They give a formula that describes the relationship between CPU and GPU rendering:

$$RT(x) = ET_{system} + \max(ET_{CPU}, ET_{GPU}), \tag{2.2}$$

which indicates that either CPU or GPU time will be the bottleneck.

Chapter 2. Related Work

They state that the actual GPU time lies somewhere between the maximum and the sum of the following terms:

$$max(C_{tv}|tv(x)|, C_f|f(x)|) \leq RT_{GPU}(x) \leq C_{tv}|tv(x)| + C_f|f(x)| \qquad (2.3)$$

$|tv(x)|$ is the number of the actually transformed vertices (i.e., the vertices not fetched from a post-transform vertex cache), which is responsible for the impact rather than the total number of primitives and vertices. Their heuristics match the experimental results sufficiently well. However, due to the limitations of the hardware functionality, they still cannot guarantee a *hard real-time system* that can fulfill the target frame rates in any case. Also, we have to keep in mind that there have again been significant changes to the hardware architectures since (e.g., unified shaders), which would require to make some adjustments to these formulas based on new measurements. Anticipating this development, Wimmer and Wonka [WW03] also mentioned a method which works independent of the current hardware architecture, based on measuring the actual rendering time.

Such a rendering time heuristics plays an important role in some of our proposed algorithms in Chapter 3. Instead of using it for online calibration of the rendering time, we use it in a preprocess to drive our view space and object space partitioning methods.

2.2 Hierarchical subdivision schemes

Hierarchical subdivision schemes have been of crucial importance for many tasks in 3D computer graphics. A huge number of variants exist for several target applications, like ray tracing, occlusion culling, or collision detection. They are commonly used as acceleration technique in order to speed up spatial searching. In ray tracing we aim to minimize the number of ray intersection tests that are required to find the intersection between the ray and the closest surface. Ideally, hierarchical subdivision schemes will break down the dependence of the rendering time on the scene complexity from

2.2. Hierarchical subdivision schemes

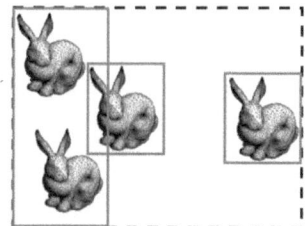 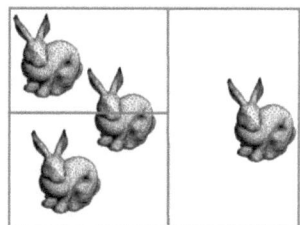

Figure 2.2: The nodes of an object hierarchies like BVH (left) can be disjoint or overlap spatially. Space subdivisions like kD-tree (right) partition the space but have to share object references between leaves.

linear ($O(N)$) to logarithmic ($O(\log(n))$). A more thorough discussion of hierarchies in the context of ray tracing can be found in the thesis of Havran et al. [Hav00]. In a slightly outdated report, Meißner et al. [MBM*01] compare the performance of different hierarchies for occlusion culling with hardware occlusion queries.

Subdivision schemes are a key element of all our visibility culling techniques. We use hierarchies to generate good view space and object space partitions during scene preprocessing in Chapter 3, and to accelerate view-frustum culling and online occlusion culling in Chapter 4.

2.2.1 Space subdivisions versus object hierarchies

Hierarchical subdivision schemes in computer graphics are either space subdivisions (or partitions) or object hierarchies (refer to Figure 2.2). Space subdivisions partition the space, and during subdivision nodes are split into two or more children separated by split planes. Hence the leaves are spatially non-overlapping. If an object does not fit into a single node, we can either allow object references to be shared between several nodes of the hierarchy, or we can split the objects along the split planes of the nodes. We generally advise to use the first option in case of real-time rendering, as object splitting can cause degeneracies, and yield many small objects which is problematic for modern GPUs.

Chapter 2. Related Work

On the other hand, multiple rendering of the same object can be avoided easily by using a simple technique called *mailboxing* (also known as ray-cache in ray tracing) [Hav00], which we use frequently in our algorithms for scene preprocessing and online culling. Mailboxing is a general technique to avoid multiple processing of the same primitive, by utilizing a global and a local counter per primitive (the "mail box"). In each pass we increase the global counter. Then we compare the mail box of each primitive to the global counter – if they have the same value the primitive has been already touched in this pass, else the primitive is processed, and the mail box is updated to the value of the global counter. Note that this simple method has to be used with caution when it comes to parallelization, because a function or thread that uses mailboxing can conflict and alter the results of other functions or threads that use mailboxing. Another option to avoid multiple references would be to allow storing objects in interior nodes, and pushing them down the tree as long as they still fully fit into the node.

On the contrary, the nodes of an object hierarchy can be spatially overlapping or disjoint, while each object belongs to exactly one leaf. Large overlapping regions near the root node can lead to decreased search efficiency of an object hierarchy compared to a spatial hierarchy and should be avoided. Widely used spatial subdivision schemes are binary space partitioning [FKN80], kD-tree, octree [Gla84], grid, and hierarchical grid. Mixed forms are also possible like B-kD tree [WMS06], or loose octree [HAM02]. We will give a short description of the most important subdivision schemes, and then describe the important surface area heuristics for node splitting.

2.2.2 Bounding volume hierarchy

Bounding volumes are a conservative approximation of the contained geometry, which they fully include. Since many years they have been used to reduce the cost of intersection queries, e.g., for ray tracing, rasterization, and collision detection [MT97]. Typical bounding volumes are axis-aligned bounding boxes (AABB), object-aligned bounding boxes (OOBB), spheres, and k-dops [KHM*98]. There is a trade-off between cost of intersection and

2.2. Hierarchical subdivision schemes

tightness of a bounding volume. Using a more complicated bounding object may pay off if it fits the actual geometry better. A GPU is optimized for sending large batches of geometry with each draw call. Hence, for algorithms where the GPU processes bounding volumes directly, more complicated bounding objects are beneficial in order to use the GPU to its full capacity – it usually does not matter if the GPU processes only six vertices of a bounding box or several times more vertices.

A *bounding volume hierarchy* (BVH) [GS87] is a hierarchy over all the individual bounding volumes, where each parent volume contains all the leaf volumes. The BVHs used in computer graphics are usually binary trees with two children. As nodes of a BVH can either overlap or be disjoint, the major strength of a BVH is its great flexibility and the ability to be modified easily. Also, because the fact that there is exactly one object reference per hierarchy, no additional memory has to be allocated for shared references during subdivision, allowing faster rebuild than most other techniques.

When used for ray tracing, traversal of a BVH is slower than traversal of a kD-tree, because of the costlier intersection test (six sides of a box versus single plane). However, BVH is an excellent alternative for ray tracing of dynamic scenes, where build time and update time of the hierarchy are dominating factors [Wal07]. BVH can handle dynamic objects very elegantly either by updating the extent of the nodes or by regenerating parts of the hierarchy. When used for rasterization, BVH seems to outperform most other techniques. It has been shown to be very efficient for occlusion culling with hardware occlusion queries [MBM*01], as it allows relatively tight bounds for objects in sparse scenes compared to e.g., octrees or even kD-trees. While kD-trees are a good choice for ray tracing because of the fast traversal times, they lose this advantage over BVH for rasterization. These are also the reasons why we generally use BVH in our algorithms whenever we have to build a hierarchy over the scene geometry, be it for preprocessing or online occlusion culling. Note that there are also algorithms for bottom-up construction of a BVH based on clustering.

Chapter 2. Related Work

2.2.3 Binary space partitioning

A *binary space partitioning* (BSP) tree is the most general of the listed spatial subdivision schemes. It has the highest degrees of freedom, as the split plane orientation can be chosen freely. Aligning the split planes with the geometry makes it possible to separate the geometry into an inside and an outside part [Tel92b]. In the past, BSP has been a widely used scheme in ray tracing and also for visibility determination in rasterization back when overdraw was very costly, and the predominant type of scenes were structured architectural scenes with straight corridors. BSP is difficult to use with nowadays' increasingly complex scenes (consider e.g., large vegetation scenes), and the gained accuracy is usually not worth the extremely time consuming task of generating an optimized BSP tree [Abr96].

2.2.4 kD-tree

A *kD-tree* can be seen as a specialization of a BSP tree, and is a good trade-off between flexibility and complexity. The split plane of a kD-tree is always axis aligned. Several heuristics exist to choose the position of the split plane, e.g., spatial median, object median, or the superior surface area heuristics [Hav00]. kD-trees have been very popular for ray tracing acceleration, as they statistically have the best performance for traversal over a large class of scenes with the Surface Area Heuristics. They have the useful ability to cut off large regions of empty space in early stages of the subdivision. The object references are usually stored in the leaf nodes that intersect the bounding box of an object (allowing multiple references). Partly because these multiple references can be quite inconvenient to handle, we use kD-tree and even BSP only for view space subdivision in our algorithms.

2.2.5 Octree

The classical *octree* divides the parent node into 8 equally spaced child nodes along all three axes. The split planes are always set to the spatial median of the node in each axis. Objects can be either stored in the leaves (allow-

2.2. Hierarchical subdivision schemes

ing multiple references), or each object is stored in the smallest node that fully contains it (allowing nodes to be stored in interior nodes). This data structure is easy to implement, fast to update, very robust in the sense that it never degenerates, and yields solid to good performance in virtually any case. However, it is less suited for scenes that are rather unevenly distributed (e.g., the famous teapot in a stadium scene) than more flexible schemes like kD-tree. Due to this inflexibility, an octree can become inefficient if objects intersect the borders between two octants early in the subdivision. In this case even small objects may end up near the root just because of their location in the tree, or have to be referenced in many octants. In the worst case, an object has to be referenced in all eight octants if it incidentally lies near the exact center of the root node.

Loose octree The *loose octree* is a variant of the octree that solves the above-mentioned problem. The additional parameter R describes the extended radius of a node. The extended radius is R times larger than the radius of the original octree node, allowing for some overlap between the nodes. In this particular octree implementation, objects belong to a single node, which can either be a leaf node or a interior node. Objects are placed into the smallest node where they still completely fit into. Setting $R = 0$ yields the original octree with no overlap between nodes. Choosing a larger R means that objects are placed deeper down the tree and less objects have to be touched. On the other hand the octree becomes "looser" (= more conservative) and more nodes have to be tested. The loose octree is an excellent data structure for fully dynamic scenes, as insertion and deletion of an object is cheap. Choosing $R = 2$ is convenient, because an object always fits fully into the extended node if it is smaller or equal in size to the original octree node. Furthermore, the hierarchy level of the node can be immediately derived from the size of the object, hence insertion can be done in $O(1)$ [HAM02]. Such a data structure is used, e.g., by the rendering engine Ogre3D [Jun06].

Chapter 2. Related Work

2.2.6 Grid and hierarchical grid

Grids are simple to implement and quick to build. During runtime the cell that contains the current view point can be found in constant time. On the downside, grids are inflexible, and choosing the right granularity for the grid is essential for a good performance. In scenes where the geometry is very unevenly distributed, a globally good granularity cannot be reached. In such a case, the more flexible hierarchical grid [CDP95] can be used. A hierarchical grid could be seen as a generalization of an octree with n children, with n being the number of grid cells in a single grid. Recently grids got renewed awareness in the context of ray tracing in dynamic scenes, because in general they do not have to be updated between frames [WIK*06].

2.2.7 Surface area heuristics

The *surface area heuristics* (SAH) [MB90] is known as the best cost model for ray-object intersections. It is used for two purposes -it decides if splitting a node is feasible or subdivision should be terminated at this point, and computes the optimal split plane position. One of the reasons for the success of kD-trees is that they can be easily optimized with SAH. This heuristics assumes a uniform distribution of rays without considering occlusion and then performs a greedy optimization. The method achieves very good results for ray tracing applications, and it is also useful for rasterization, where the view frustum can be seen as a beam of rays. The estimated cost for a node after the split into a left child C_l and a right child C_r is

$$C = p_l C_l + p_r C_r, \qquad (2.4)$$

where p is the probability that the child node will be traversed given that the parent node is traversed, which is equal to the ratio of the surface area A of the child node to the surface area of the parent node, hence the formula can be written as

$$C = \frac{A_l C_l + A_r C_r}{A}. \qquad (2.5)$$

2.3. Methods for rendering simplification

Intuitively, one of the strengths of SAH is that it cuts off regions of empty space very soon. The decision to further subdivide a node is based on the ratio of the estimated cost of the parent node and the estimated costs of the child nodes. The candidates for split planes in a kD-tree node are induced by the bounding boxes of the primitives, because there can be no maximum of the cost function in between. Building a tree with SAH requires $O(n \log(n))$ time if the split plane candidates are pre-sorted globally, but faster approximations exist [HMS06]. SAH is not restricted to kD-trees, and has been successfully used with other schemes like BVH.

2.3 Methods for rendering simplification

2.3.1 Level of detail

Level of detail (LOD) denotes the representation of an object using different levels of simplification. It is based on the assumption that under certain conditions a simplified version of an object provides sufficient rendering quality. In early years *geometric* LOD was predominantly used. Nowadays it is as important to have other forms of LODs like *shader level of detail*, where a single material contains several shader versions with varying complexity, and *detail textures* for extreme close-ups. Most commonly, the appropriate LOD level is chosen based on the distance to the view point. Perceptually it is very important that the transitions between different LOD levels stay unnoticed.

Geometric level of detail can be either discrete or continuous. Continuous level of detail was a vivid research area for many years [Hop96]. However, it is rarely used in practice because developers rather want to have full control over the LOD representations at any time. Furthermore, techniques like edge collapse are inefficient on modern GPUs.

Discrete LODs are easier to handle than continuous LODs, but suffer from distracting popping artifacts in the moment when they make a so called hard switch between two representations. There are different ways to avoid these artifacts. Delaying the switch until there no visual difference between the two representations (so-called *late-switching*) completely removes popping

Chapter 2. Related Work

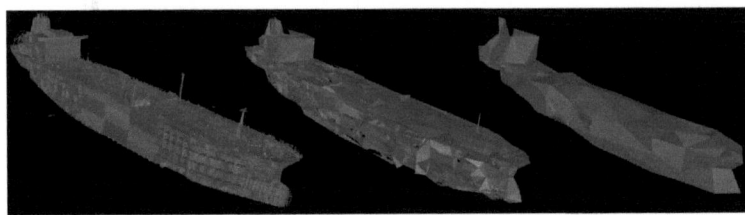

Figure 2.3: Hierarchical LODs of the DoubleEagle tanker model. Image courtesy of Erikson et al. [EMWVB01].

artifacts, but does not offer enough potential for rendering acceleration. It is more useful to have smooth blending between subsequent LOD levels [GW07, SW08], which makes the transition much less noticeable.

Using traditional LOD generation for the simplification of highly complex models is suboptimal for rendering on modern GPUs, because many low-poly models must be handled as separate entities. Another disadvantage of traditional LODs is that each object is simplified separately on a local level, but no attention is given to the global appearance. Erikson et al. [EMWVB01] avoid these drawbacks using *hierarchical level of detail* (HLOD). The method simplifies the geometry on a global level, keeping the highest (i.e., most detailed) LODs in the leaf nodes. Using a bottom-up construction with the constraint that all LOD levels should have roughly the same number of triangles that is optimal for the given GPU, the method combines and simplifies the geometry contained in the two child nodes before storing it in the parent node. An example of HLOD of the DoubleEagle tanker model can be seen in Figure 2.3.

2.3.2 Image-based rendering

Unlike standard 3D rendering, which renders from geometry, *image-based rendering* (IBR) renders directly from images. Skipping the whole transformation pipeline, image based approaches can accelerate rendering significantly. On the downside, they may require a lot of texture memory and precomputation time, and it is nontrivial to handle several features that are

2.3. Methods for rendering simplification

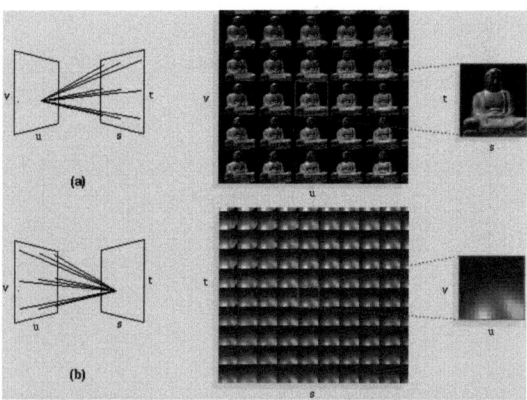

Figure 2.4: The 4D light field describes the radiance on a ray between any two points. Images are 2D slices of the 4D light field. Image courtesy of Levoy et al. [LH96a].

taken for granted when working with real geometry, like dynamic scenes, depth, or relighting.

The most extreme form of image based rendering is the 4D light field [LH96a], also known as the Lumigraph [GGSC96], where images are treated as 2D slices of a 4D function. This function describes the radiance of a ray between any 2 points on the two planes that parametrize the light field (refer to Figure 2.4). This approach allowed to render complex objects and environments at real-time frame rates back in 1996, but has an enormously high memory footprint and limited degree of freedom.

IBR rendering is commonly used in combination with actual geometry in the form of *impostors* or *billboards*, based on the assumption that geometry can be represented reasonably well by images within certain constraints [Jes05]. When moving through the scene, the images will eventually become invalid (i.e., their approximation error becomes too high), and they have to be updated accordingly. Good candidates for billboards are far away objects that change their appearance slowly, e.g., the sun, the sky, or a distant background. The parallax error of impostors can be reduced with

Chapter 2. Related Work

layered depth images [SGHS98].

The image cache [SLS*96, SS96] algorithm constructs a scene hierarchy and keeps cached images of nodes on different hierarchy levels. Due to temporal coherence, the images can be reused for a certain lifespan. The method automatically updates nodes corresponding to invalidated regions, based on an error metric that quantifies the difference between the cached image and the real appearance. However, the technique requires a high amount of texture memory and frequent updates if the constraints are very strict.

The high memory requirements of impostors were addressed by Jeschke et al. [JWS02]. They aim to reach a desired target frame rate and image quality using automatic impostors placement, while keeping the texture memory consumption low. For optimal performance, they use impostors in combination with conservative visibility culling and geometric LODs.

Impostors are well suited to fill up holes resulting from aggressive visibility culling. This approach is useful for dense forest scenes, where trees in the background are only visible through small holes in the foreground [SLCO*04]. See Section 2.4.4 for an overview of hybrid methods that combine IBR, LODs, and visibility culling.

Billboard clouds [DDSD03] represent geometry as a set of billboards that are oriented according to some similarity heuristics. Billboard clouds combine the strengths of mesh decimation and IBR, allowing automatic simplification within a given error bound. Billboard clouds have been successfully used for approximating complex geometry with high frequencies like trees [MHMT05], but are less useful for representing regular structures like buildings.

Normal mapping is a technique that simulates surface details on simple or simplified geometry. Appearance-preserving simplification [COM98] can be done by storing the high-frequency normals of the detailed model in a *normal map*, and using this map to illuminate the surface instead of the actual normal of the simplified model. The illusion breaks at the silhouettes of objects. Parallax mapping [KTI*01] displaces texture coordinates according to a height map, which gives a better impression of the parallax effect and depth perception. Using a generalization of relief mapping, non-height-field mesostructures like weaves can be represented with minimal

2.4. Visibility culling

distortions [PO06]. At the cost of longer rendering times, a correct parallax effect, self occlusion, and silhouettes can be achieved [JMW07].

2.4 Visibility culling

In this section we discuss one of the core topics of this thesis, methods that aim to detect the visible parts of the scene as early as possible. For a general overview of visibility culling please refer to the excellent surveys of Cohen-Or et al. [COCSD02] and Bittner and Wonka [BW03].

Many classifications of visibility algorithms exist in literature. Some of them seem to be outdated, like the classification according to the dimensionality – nowadays 2D and 2.5D visibility problems are mostly solved and lost their significance as a research problem. In this survey we instead focus on techniques that are able to handle arbitrary 3D scenes. Naturally visibility preprocessing algorithms compute visibility from one or multiple *regions* in space (otherwise we would have to deal with an infinite number of view points), whereas online occlusion culling algorithms calculate visibility from a single view *point*. Hence we use the straightforward distinction into algorithms for visibility preprocessing and algorithms for online occlusion culling.

First we investigate algorithms that partition the object space and view space of a scene, which is a necessary preparation for subsequent visibility culling. Then we discuss algorithms for visibility preprocessing, and afterwards algorithms for online culling. At last we discuss algorithms that combine visibility culling with other acceleration techniques like LODs and IBR.

2.4.1 Methods for scene preprocessing

Given a scene that consists purely of a triangle soup, we first have to partition the view space into regions in space, so called view cells, and the object space into meaningful entities. Only afterwards we can apply algorithms that find the potentially visible objects for each view cell. The quality of scene prepro-

Chapter 2. Related Work

cessing will have a large influence on the efficiency of the PVS computation, and during runtime on PVS-based rendering in terms of rendering time and memory cost. The following part of our survey discusses algorithms for scene preprocessing, which are previous work for our scene processing algorithms in Chapter 3.

View space subdivision techniques for view cell generation have been used in visibility preprocessing from the very beginning, whereas objects are often assumed to be already given, e.g., designed by an artist. An automatic object construction is useful in the case that no objects are given a priori, or if the given objects are suboptimal for visibility culling (e.g., too large or of uneven sizes). Note that it is always infeasible to use a triangle soup directly for rendering, because modern GPUs prefer many primitives per rendering call for optimal performance. It would also require a huge amount of memory to store the triangle-based PVSs of all view cells. First we give an overview of algorithms for view space subdivision, then we discuss the few papers that cover object space partitioning.

2.4.1.1 View space partitioning

The first visibility preprocessing methods were designed for accelerating walk-throughs of indoor architectural environments [ARB90, TS91]. These methods partition the scene into cells roughly corresponding to rooms in the building. The cells are connected by portals which correspond to transparent boundaries between the cells.

Airey et al.[ARB90] defined a set of rules which the view space subdivision algorithm should satisfy. They construct a kD-tree where the subdivision planes are aligned with scene polygons. For each candidate plane they compute its priority as a weighted sum of its occlusion properties and the estimated balance and size of the tree. A similar technique was used by Teller and Séquin [TS91], and was later extended to an auto-partition BSP tree [Tel92b].

As noticed by Teller [Tel92b], in general 3D scenes with non-axial polygons, the subdivision may result in cell fragmentation. This problem was

2.4. Visibility culling

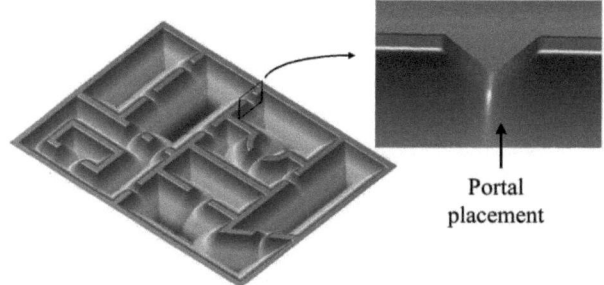

Portal placement

Figure 2.5: Haumond et al. use a watershed algorithm on a distance field to compute view cells. The portals are set to the saddle points where two cells meet. Image courtesy of Haumond et al. [HDS03].

addressed by Meneveaux et al. [MBMD98], who focused on building interiors. In the first step they extract the floors of the building, and in the second step they use a 2D method to partition each floor separately. The 2D method clusters candidate splitting planes in dual space to find those planes which provide the best fit to the walls of the building.

Despite the research on constructing cell and portal graphs, the manual construction of cells and portals during the modeling phase is still considered a valuable option especially for indoor maze-like scenes [LG95b, Ail00].

Lerner et al. designed an algorithm which aims to create short portals [LCOC03]. The algorithm is suitable for 2D scenes and 2.5D scenes with buildings of comparable height. The authors also present a cost model for evaluating the efficiency of the resulting partition. Using this cost model, it is shown that the method delivers superior partitions compared to previous BSP tree based algorithms. As all view cells have the same user defined height, the efficiency of the algorithm is highly dependent on this parameter. Also, the resulting partition lacks any kind of horizontal separation, which from our experience is very important in outdoor scenes.

Haumont et al. [HDS03] chose a significantly different strategy for constructing a cell and portal graph. They use a voxelization of the scene and the watershed algorithm computed on a distance field. The method grows

Chapter 2. Related Work

cells from local minima of the distance field and introduces portals when two cells meet (refer to Figure 2.5). Similarly to the method of Lerner et al. [LCOC03], this approach uses a top-down subdivision (voxelization) as well as a localized bottom-up cell construction (watershed).

All the methods mentioned above deal with the construction of cell and portal graphs. The PVS concept has been used by numerous methods which do not need portals for PVS computation [COCSD02]. Most of these methods focus only on the PVS determination step, i.e., computing from-region visibility. They assume that the view cells are either defined by the user or use a simple view space subdivision without further considerations.

However, there are several methods which indirectly deal with the problem of finding a good set of view cells. Additionally, unlike the above-mentioned cell and portal methods, they make use of the actual visibility information [GSF99, SVNB99, vdPS99, NB04a].

Van de Panne and Stewart [vdPS99] designed a compression scheme for PVSs computed for a set of view cells. As a side-product of the compression, some cells get merged.

Gotsman et al. [GSF99] construct a 5D subdivision of view space in the spatial and angular domain corresponding to the position and direction of viewing rays. They use sampled visibility to evaluate the efficiency of the candidate splitting planes using the following heuristics for the efficiency of a split of node n into child nodes l and r:

$$Eff(l,r) = \left(\frac{1-|PVS(l)\cap|PVS(r)|}{|PVS(n)|}\right)\left(\frac{1-|V(l)\cap|V(r)|}{|V(n)|}\right), \quad (2.6)$$

where the first term emphasizes the difference in the PVSs, and the second the tree balance in terms of 5D volumes V. The split candidates in the spatial domain are induced by the bounding boxes of the objects. Unfortunately, the authors give no hint in the paper of how to choose split candidates in the angular domain. To reduce the high storage requirements they suggest to store the PVSs in bitsets, setting bit i to 1 if the object i is in the PVS,

2.4. Visibility culling

to 0 otherwise.

The visibility octree of Saona-Vázquez et al. [SVNB99] is constructed by a view space subdivision which terminates when reaching a predefined triangle budget or when visibility cannot be reduced by the associated conservative algorithm. Similarly to Saona-Vázquez et al. [SVNB99], Nirenstein and Blake [NB04a] use a hierarchical view space subdivision which is terminated if the desired triangle budget is reached. Using aggressive visibility sampling, the triangle budget is determined from the PVS computed for the view cell.

The view cell determination in all these methods is driven by rather simple models which consider only PVS set differences. Additionally the methods of Gotsman et al., Saona-Vázquez et al. and Nirenstein and Blake perform only top-down view space subdivision, which need not adapt well to local visibility changes. On the other hand the method of van de Panne and Stewart performs only bottom-up construction, which does not permit using a larger number of initial view cells. In comparison, our method for view cell construction 3.4 aims to give a deeper analysis of finding a good set of view cells based on actual visibility. We provide a new cost model for evaluating the efficiency of the constructed view cells. The model is based on the estimated render cost for a given view space partition. Also, it does not provide only a fixed set of view cells. Instead it constructs a novel form of view cell hierarchy from which we can extract an optimized set of view cells for a given memory budget.

2.4.1.2 Object space partitioning

Creating a set of objects from a triangle soup can be done using top-down (subdivision) or bottom-up algorithms (clustering or merging), or a combination of those. Clustering algorithms are usually quite slow, hence subdivision algorithms like kD-tree or BVH have been predominantly used in the past for different applications like ray tracing, occlusion culling, and collision detection, with some exceptions.

The method of Baxter at al. [BSGM02] partitions the given geometry

Chapter 2. Related Work

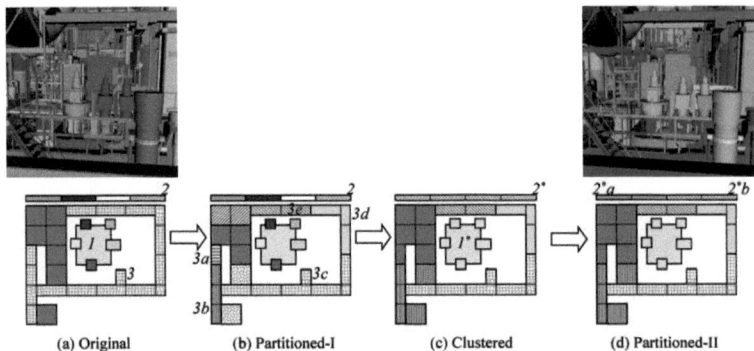

Figure 2.6: Baxter et al. redefine the given objects for optimal (occlusion culling) performance. Top row: (left) original objects, (right) new objects. Bottom row: (a) original objects (b) partitioning into smaller objects, (c) clustering step, (d) repartitioning to avoid uneven clusters. Image courtesy of Baxter et al. [BSGM02].

into smaller objects based on size, aspect ratios, and polygon count. Then the algorithm clusters the objects in a bottom-up fashion, using the heuristics that the Hausdorff distance between objects inside of a cluster should be smaller than the distance to objects outside of the cluster. In a final refinement step, the method repartitions the clusters mainly based on their aspect ratio, in order to avoid clusters with uneven distributions of objects. Refer to Figure 2.6 to see all stages of the algorithm, which was successfully applied for online visibility computations. However, it is not obvious how to use the method for optimizing subdivisions for preprocessed visibility.

Another clustering method for online visibility has been proposed by Kortenjan and Schomaker [KS06]. The most important idea of their work is that they construct an object space subdivision so that the nodes of the subdivision maintain not only spatial locality but also contain geometry of comparable size.

2.4. Visibility culling

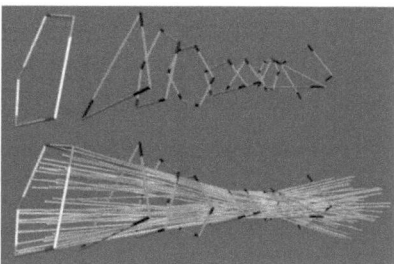

Figure 2.7: Extremal stabbing lines through a series of portals. Image courtesy of Teller et al. [Tel92a].

2.4.2 Visibility preprocessing

Once we have a meaningful partitioning into view cells and objects, it is the responsibility of a visibility preprocessing algorithm to associate the objects with the view cell from which they are visible and store them in the potentially visible set (PVS) of the particular view cell. Visibility preprocessing has been an important topic of research since about 20 years. PVS-based rendering causes practically no runtime overhead – the only task involved is to locate the current view cell. Therefore preprocessing was the only practical choice until hardware occlusion queries became suitable for real time usage, and hence we will discuss a number of relatively old algorithms in the following which are nevertheless still of interest. However, the high complexity of from-region visibility makes preprocessing a challenging problem in the general case up to this day. In this survey, we keep the classical separation into geometric algorithms that compute conservative or exact visibility, and sampling-based algorithms that compute aggressive visibility.

2.4.2.1 Geometric algorithms

The earliest proposed methods were geometric algorithms that operate in object space, which means that their complexity is proportional to the geometric complexity of the used models, and they are either *exact* or *conservative* in nature. A non-trivial problem for all geometric methods is the handling of

Chapter 2. Related Work

occluder fusion, which requires special treatment.

Exact 3D visibility The *aspect graph* [GM90] is a tool that connects qualitatively (i.e., topologically) different 2D views (i.e., aspects) of a polygonal scene. A change of aspects happens due so-called *visual events*. The two fundamental visual events are (a) when the projections of a vertex and an edge coincide and (b) when the projections of 3 edges meet in a point. It is the dual of the *viewpoint space partition*, which encodes the maximal regions with a constant aspect. It is the finest possible encoding of the view space and is able to answer all visibility queries, but has the enormously high complexity of n^9 in the worst case.

The 3D visibility complex encodes a partition into *maximal free line segments* (i.e., the line segments between the extremal points of the bounding objects). The more lightweight visibility skeleton [Dur99] only encodes the visual events, but still has a complexity of $O(n^4)$. These algorithms are very complex and only of interest for the analysis of visibility properties.

The duality of shadows and visibility was exploited by Teller et al. [Tel92a]. They compute visibility through a series of convex portals in $O(n^2)$ time, using the notion of *antipenumbra*, which is just the volume from where a part but not all of the last in a sequence of portals (which could be interpreted as a light source) can be seen. The method uses a Plücker space representation to compute the antipenumbra. A Plücker parametrization of the edges yields hyperplanes that define a 5D polytope. The polytope is intersected with the 4D Plücker quadric to find the dual of all *extremal stabbing lines* (i.e., lines that stab all polygons and are fixed by four edges) and the corresponding extremal swaths, which are either planes or quadratic surfaces (refer to Figure 2.7). This idea was later used for robust soft shadow computation, introducing *epsilon* visibility [DD02].

All aforementioned algorithms in this section are infeasible for classical visibility preprocessing in a 3D scene. Bittner [Bit03] proposes the first *tractable* solution suitable for small and medium sized 3D scenes. Using a mapping from primal space to Plücker coordinates, he maintains a compact representation of the union of the blocker polyhedra in an 5D BSP tree,

2.4. Visibility culling

denoted as occlusion tree. Several other exact visibility algorithms were proposed that are conceptually very similar [NBG02, HMN05, MAM05].

These exact algorithms give valuable insight into the properties of visibility and are conceptually interesting – at least theoretically one of the oldest problems of computer graphics has been solved – but they can hardly be extended to efficiently and robustly handle visibility preprocessing in large scenes. In fact it was shown that sampling-based algorithms like GVS can compute more accurate PVSs [WWZ*06]

Simplification of the problem domain Several papers were proposed that made simplifying assumptions to reduce the complexity of the problem. These methods either specialize on a specific scene configuration like indoor or city scenes, or restrict their methods to solve simple visibility configurations, while accepting an overestimation of the PVSs.

In the beginning, the authors focussed only on architectural scenes, exploiting the beneficial cell and portal structure [ARB90, TS91], where the cells are usually rooms which can see each other only through portals, i.e., doors or windows. Airey et al. [ARB90] suggest two solution to compute the PVS: an aggressive algorithm that uses point sampling, and a conservative algorithm that uses shadow volumes to find the visible objects.

Many authors exploit the predominantly flat nature of some scenes like, e.g., city scenarios or terrains, and reduce the problem complexity to so-called 2.5D visibility [WWS00, BWW01, KCCO01, BWW05]. The 2D algorithm of Wonka et al. [WWS00] shrinks occluders to enlarge the valid range of from-point visibility to areas within an ϵ environment around a point sample. Occluder fusion can be handled by testing objects against the joint umbra of shrunk occluders.

Later several algorithms have been proposed that can handle 3D outdoor scenarios [COFHZ98, LSCO03, DDTP00, LSCO03]. With the exception of the algorithm of Cohen-Or et al. [COFHZ98], all these algorithms support occluder fusion, mostly based on merging separate occluder umbrae into a larger conjoint umbra. Unfortunately, they rely on occlusion mostly due to larger occluders close to the view cell, and can be arbitrarily wrong in terms

Chapter 2. Related Work

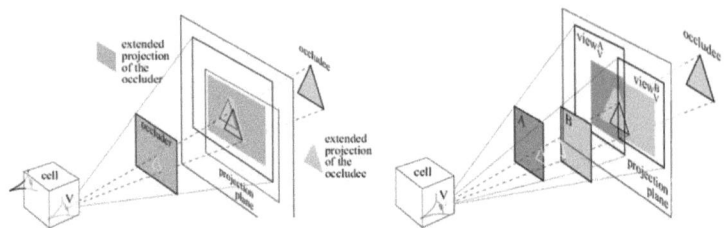

Figure 2.8: (left) Extended projections use the intersection of occluder projections and the union of occludee projections for conservative per-view cell visibility. (right) The green triangle can be culled using occluder fusion. Image courtesy of Durand et al. [DDTP00].

of PVS size overestimation.

Cohen-Or et al. [COFHZ98] use a rectangular grid of view cells. An object A is called a *strong occluder* of another object B if it occludes B from every point on a view cell, in other words, B fully lies in the umbra of A as induced by the view cell. The methods searches a single strong occluder for each view cell and object. Casting a ray from every vertex of the view cell to every vertex of the polyhedron, they list every object intersected by the ray as potential occluder. An object is a strong occluder iff the intersection of these sets is non-empty.

Extended projections [DDTP00] are conceptually very interesting, as they can be seen as a generalization of occlusion maps known from image-based from-point visibility to a per-region visibility problem. The extended projection of an occluder is defined as the *intersection* of the projections from any point in a view cell, while the projection of an occludee is defined as the *union* of the projections from any point in the view cell (refer to Figure 2.8), always maintaining conservativity. Occluder fusion is possible by intersecting the projections of several occluders. However, the tightness of the PVS is highly dependent on the location of the projection planes. An *occlusion sweep* that reprojects the occluder projection onto a new plane and merges it with new occluders provides an improvement in some cases.

Leyvand et al. [LSCO03] also use the assumption that due to gravity

2.4. Visibility culling

most scenes have approximately a 2.5D nature, or as they call it, 3-ϵD. They factorize a 4D from-region visibility problem into a vertical and a more important horizontal component. In the horizontal direction they use ray-space factorization, and they use umbra merging in the vertical direction.

Schaufler et al. [SDDS00] create a discrete representation of the scene in order to make visibility computation independent of the scene complexity. They classify voxels as empty, border (if they contain a boundary), or opaque, and restrict their method to use the opaque interior of scenes as volumetric occluders. The method uses blocker extension into adjacent opaque regions to maximize occlusion and constructs shafts between view cell and blockers (i.e., the umbras) that extend blockers into empty space, allowing efficient occluder fusion. One of the advantages of volumetric visibility is that it can be used to cull anything that is completely inside hidden space, including moving objects.

To our knowledge none of the introduced geometric methods can handle all possible scene configurations. For example, all of them have problems with large vegetation scenes, which are inherently difficult to process sufficiently well in terms of both performance and accuracy of the PVSs.

2.4.2.2 Sampling-based algorithms

Many people in the research community considered preprocessed visibility to be solved after the first tractable exact visibility algorithms had been proposed. However, these algorithms cannot be applied on large and complex scenes. Many geometric solutions suffer from all kinds of drawbacks, be it performance, accuracy, tightness of the PVS, or applicability. Due to their robustness and simplicity, game studios have been using primitive sampling-based algorithms instead of geometric methods for years, and there was a huge gap of available scientific algorithms and the demands of the industry. Hence sampling-based algorithms that sample ray space very densely got renewed attention in the scientific community in recent years, with the main focus on more intelligent sampling strategies. These algorithms are inherently *aggressive* or *approximate* in nature.

Chapter 2. Related Work

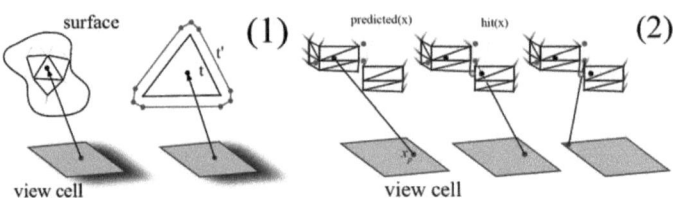

Figure 2.9: Guided visibility sampling uses two powerful techniques: (1) Adaptive-border sampling mutates the end point of a successful ray to find new triangles in the neighborhood. (2) Reverse sampling mutates the starting point of a ray so that it goes through the predicted end point shown in yellow. Image courtesy of Wonka et al. [WWZ*06].

The conceptually simplest idea is to shoot random rays from a view cell [ARB90, SGwHS98]. In order to reduce the complexity of the problem domain by one dimension, it is beneficial to first sample the boundary of the view cell with points and then sample visibility from each of these points [LH96b, Stu99]. Recent algorithms try to address the question on how to best position new samples based on visibility information from previous samples [Pit99, GSF99, WM03, NB04b, WWZ*06]. We describe the algorithm of Wonka et al. [WWZ*06] as an example for this class of algorithms, that uses rather simple but very efficient concepts for intelligent sample placement.

Guided Visibility Sampling (GVS) GVS [WWZ*06] accelerates the computation of a triangle-based PVS from a view cell by sampling only a subset of ray space. The algorithm avoids sampling triangles that have already been found or to sample empty space, and concentrates on sampling the unexplored border regions and gaps instead.

GVS starts all samples from the borders of a view cell. It initially casts a certain number of random samples into the scene. If such a sample successfully finds a new triangle, it is used as seeding ray for subsequent ray mutations. The efficiency of the algorithm comes from only two different ray mutation techniques, *adaptive border sampling*, and *reverse sampling*. Adap-

2.4. Visibility culling

tive border sampling exploits the connectivity of meshes. It searches the border of newly found triangles within some ϵ environment for more triangles by mutating the end point of a successful ray (see Figure 2.9 (1)). If the algorithm detects a discontinuity by comparing the end point of the current ray to the predicted end point, it uses reverse sampling to explore the gap. It mutates the starting point of the current ray so that it goes through the predicted end point, which is just the intersection of the current ray with the plane of the triangle hit by the previous ray (see Figure 2.9 (2)).

GVS computes a very accurate PVS in the range of a few seconds per view cell for large models like the Powerplant. The method is also very memory efficient, and no complicated auxiliary structure is required for the algorithm itself, only the current PVS as well as a buffer containing the candidates for ray mutation to indicate the current state of computation.

Until now all introduced methods compute visibility only for a *single* view cell at a time, and timings in the papers are usually only given for computation of a single view cell. However, in practice we have to deal with several thousand view cells per scene, hence there is a large multiplicative factor involved when estimating the time it takes to compute a full visibility solution for all view cells. If the PVS differences between neighbouring view cells are small, then such a visibility algorithm is highly inefficient.

Laine et al. [Lai05] were the first who exploit the high degree of coherence between view cells, by propagating visibility over view cell borders towards neighbouring view cells. The algorithm has been verified to work in combination with different types of visibility solvers. The authors showed how to create a directed graph that allows unambiguous propagation of visibility between view cells without creating loops.

Adaptive Global Visibility Sampling (AGVS) AGVS [BMW*09] fully exploits spatial coherence between view cells using a powerful global sampling approach, and allows progressive refinement of the visibility solution. AGVS was the first full fledged PVS computation algorithm which exploits global sampling [MBW06] for their use. In order to compute visibility for all view cells at the same time, the method creates maximal free line segments be-

Chapter 2. Related Work

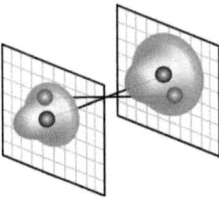

Figure 2.10: The AGVS algorithm uses a two-point mutation which shifts the end points of a ray according to a Gaussian distribution. Image courtesy of Bittner et al. [BMW*09].

tween two objects. The objects are then are added to the PVSs of *all* view cells that are intersected by the segments.

The authors propose a number of efficient global sampling strategies. They distinguish between so called *static* and *stochastic* sample distributions. Static sample distributions denote random sampling schemes that do not depend on the success of recent samples. Examples for static sample distributions are: a point-direction distribution, which defines a sample with a point in view space and a direction, or a point-point distribution, which defines a sample with two points in view space. The latter strategy is suited for scenes that are not uniformly shaped, like more or less all city scenes that have relatively small extent in the vertical direction compared to the other dimensions.

Stochastic sample distributions are based on the mutation of successful rays, which are those that bring a new *contribution* in form of a new PVS entry. A number of successful rays are stored in a mutation buffer and subsequently used to drive the mutations. AGVS uses 3 types of ray mutations: (1) The two-point mutation is the simplest but probably most powerful technique that mutates the end points of a ray segment according to a Gaussian distribution, as shown in Figure 2.10. (2) Silhouette rays use fast rejection sampling to find the silhouettes of objects. (3) Reverse sampling mutates only the origin of rays. Note that the latter two techniques have their deterministic counterparts in the GVS algorithm. Ray distributions are chosen with a probability proportional to their average contribution.

2.4. Visibility culling

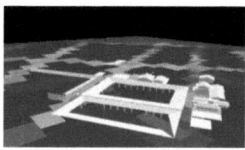

Figure 2.11: Interactive visibility analysis with the AGVS algorithm. (left) A view cell in the Pompeii scene. (middle) A visualization of the render cost in the view cells that are on the same level as the current view cell (warmer colors mean higher cost). (right) Over the roofs we have so called visibility hotspots with very high render cost. Image courtesy of Bittner et al. [BMW*09].

AGVS computes visibility on a per-object granularity, because all view cells are processed in parallel, and it is impossible to keep the visible triangles in memory for all PVSs at the same time. The fact that object-based visibility is slightly more conservative than triangle-based visibility is not a big drawback, because it is inefficient to render single triangles anyway. AGVS has been shown to compute a full visibility solution several times faster than other methods. In our experience, the stochastic sampling strategies of AGVS are more robust than the deterministic strategies of GVS. Moreover, GVS might spend a long time on a single view cell if the termination criteria are set too tight, while the progressiveness of AGVS allows much better control over the appropriate time for termination.

Due to its progressiveness the method is not restricted to merely using the final solution for standard visibility culling. It can be used for interactive render cost analysis, as it is possible to get a quick preview of global visibility within some seconds (refer to Figure 2.11). In order to use AGVS for interactive scene editing, the visibility changes after an edit (e.g., an object insertion or removal) must be incorporated as efficiently as possible. Hence the method recomputes visibility only for those objects that potentially changed their status from visible to invisible. As newly inserted objects can act as an occluder, shadow volumes are constructed for all view cells to find and locally invalidate PVS entries that lie in the umbra of a new object. Finding objects that are newly visible is conveniently handled by the ray

Chapter 2. Related Work

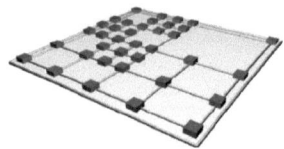

Figure 2.12: 2D visualization of the rasterization-based sampling algorithm of Nirenstein et al. The method computes visibility with hemicubes and adaptively subdivides the sampling domain based on the PVS differences of the 4 corner samples. Image courtesy of Nirenstein et al. [NB04b].

mutations that automatically focus on the regions of change.

GPU sampling Several conservative and aggressive methods exploit the rasterization capacities of the GPU to efficiently sample visibility in a regular fashion.

The algorithm of Nirenstein et al. [NB04b] is especially designed for efficient GPU-based sampling. The method samples the visibility from view cell borders with hemicubes. In order to adaptively increase the sampling density in undersampled regions, they use hierarchical subdivision. The decision for further subdivision is based on the visibility discrepancies of corner samples, as can be seen in Figure 2.12. However, this approach is inherently prone to miss small features that are not captured by the coarser sampling, and has indeed been shown to miss many visible triangles [WWZ*06] in practice. Also, such a brute force GPU-based approach has the disadvantage that the complexity scales linear with the scene size. It is a question if GPU sampling can be used to accelerate more sophisticated sampling-based algorithms like AGVS because of various potential problems, e.g., how to incorporate stochastic sampling, or how to overcome the limits of the texture memory in very large scenes.

GPU-based rasterization is also used to accelerate several conservative algorithms, where a pixel is seen as small subset of the ray space, and occlusion is reported only if the whole subset of rays is blocked [WWS00, KCCO01, LSCO03, DDTP00]. These methods are not able to handle complex visibility configurations induced by many occluders within such a pixel, and require a

2.4. Visibility culling

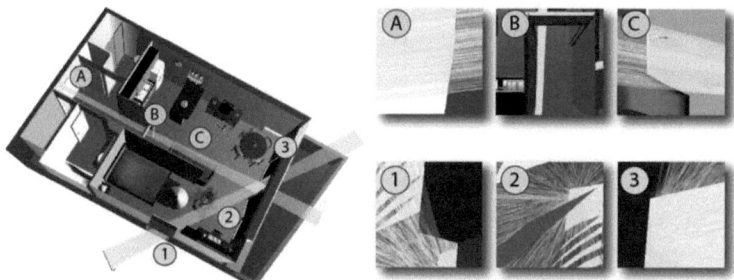

Figure 2.13: Interactive visibility analysis using the method of Eisemann et al. Two unblocked shafts of rays are visualized. The close-ups show that visibility is accurately captured. Image courtesy of Eisemann et al. [ED07].

single occluder or a fused occluder that blocks all rays.

Eisemann et al. [ED07] propose an algorithm that exploits the bitwise arithmetic abilities of modern graphics hardware with DirectX10 for computing the visibility between two patches entirely on the GPU. The method traverses all triangles, backprojects them on the light source from the receiver point, and keeps track of the number of light source samples that are occluded. Using a bitmask, the algorithm efficiently determines how many light source samples are to the left of each of the 3 oriented triangle edges, which means that they are occluded. The approach can be used for a range of applications, for example soft shadow rendering. It is physically more correct than state-of-the-art methods like single sample soft shadows [GBP06], and free of typical single-sample artifacts. However, it is significantly slower performance-wise, and hence infeasible for real-time shadows. The most promising application of this technique is visibility analysis in games (which is also the reason why we listed the method among the preprocessing algorithms in this survey). Using this functionality, a game designer is able to interactively detect visibility leaks through which objects become visible that shouldn't, causing frame-rate drops or line-of-sight problems that change the gameplay in an unwanted way. Figure 2.13 shows an example of such an assisted visibility analysis.

Chapter 2. Related Work

2.4.3 Online occlusion culling

In this section we investigate algorithms for online occlusion culling. These algorithms do not require a lengthy preprocessing step, are potentially more accurate than preprocessing as they compute visibility from a point, and can handle fully dynamic scenes. Most online culling algorithms operate in image space, hence they naturally support occluder fusion due to rasterization. They are mostly conservative in nature, using simple proxy geometry like bounding boxes to query the visibility of the actual geometry, and rely on the z-buffer [Cat75] to resolve the final visibility. Only some methods exist which compute approximate or conservative visibility.

The hierarchical z-buffer algorithm [Gre94] uses a 2-fold hierarchy to reduce the number of depth comparisons of the classical z-buffer. This method subdivides the object space into an octree hierarchy, and utilizes a z-pyramid for the depth test, which is a quad-tree hierarchy that has the original z-buffer as finest level, and each of the higher levels stores the farthest z-value of its 4 children. The octree is traversed in front-to-back order, and its nodes are tested hierarchically against the z-pyramid. If the closest z-value of a polygon is still farther away than the z-value of the current pyramid entry, it is ensured that none of its fragments can be visible, and the node can be culled. This clever algorithm introduces the important concept of *hierarchical* culling, but suffered from missing hardware support.

Hierarchical occlusion maps (HOM) [ZMHH97] are somewhat similar to the hierarchical z-buffer, as they also tests objects against an image hierarchy. The HOM algorithm makes use of the optimized texture mapping and downsampling functionality of modern graphics hardware for efficient approximate culling. To determine visibility of an object, this method performs both an overlap test and a depth test. First an object is tested against an *occlusion map* for overlap with occluders. If the object is positively tested for overlap, it is subsequently tested against a so called *depth estimation buffer*, which conservatively estimates the occluded depth using the farthest z-value of an occluder. An occlusion map is a grayscale image that is part of an occlusion pyramid. The pyramid is created by rendering a number of occluders into

2.4. Visibility culling

Figure 2.14: This image shows the generation of n-buffers. (1) Level 0 is the depth buffer. (2) Level 1 stores the maximal values of 2x2 pixel neighborhoods in the depth buffer (e.g., the highlighted entry corresponds to the pixels in the red box in level 0). (3) Level 2 stores the maximal values of 4x4 pixels (e.g., magenta box). (4) Likewise, level 3 for 8x8 pixels (e.g., yellow box). Image courtesy of Décoret et al. [Déc05].

such an occlusion map, and then using the downsampling functionality of the GPU to build the other levels. These grayscale images can then be used for approximate culling with an alpha threshold. The algorithm is historically important and contributed valuable ideas, like the efficient generation of the occlusion maps using texture hardware. However, in my opinion it became more or less outdated since the introduction of hardware occlusion queries.

Approximate culling is also used by a class of methods known as stress culling in the literature [Won01]. These methods aim to render in the best quality possible while staying within the constraints of a given rendering budget, like the Prioritized-Layered Projection (PLP) algorithm [KS00]. This algorithm prioritizes geometry based on its so called *solidity* value, which corresponds to the likelihood of being occluded. Next the method simply renders the geometry ordered by their priority until a certain memory budget is reached. While the original algorithm does not bother to fill up the holes that appear due to their aggressive culling, a conservative extension of the algorithm exists [KS01].

N-Buffers are an interesting data structure proposed by Décoret et al. [Déc05]. A couple of depth maps are stored similar to an image pyramid or mip-maps, but with the difference that all depth maps have the same size. The pixel (x,y) of the depth map of level i stores the maximum depth value of a $2^i x 2^i$ neighbourhood of pixels. An example of n-buffers can be seen in Figure 2.14.

Chapter 2. Related Work

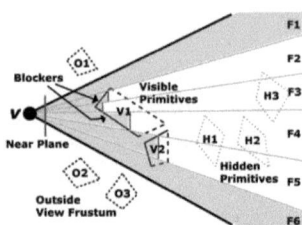

Figure 2.15: The conservative from-point algorithm of Chandak et al. subdivides the view frustrum, and adjusts the far plane of the sub-frustra if there is a single occluder that fully blocks them. Image courtesy of Chandak et al. [CATM09].

A rectangular region is queried against the level with the smallest i where the pixel neighbourhood corresponding to an entry fully contains the region. According to the authors, the projection of any object can be covered reasonably tightly with 4 power-of-two squares. Hence, an object of any size and orientation can be queried for visibility with a constant overhead of 4 lookups into the occlusion maps.

N-buffers have larger memory requirements than mip-maps, but they are more flexible, and were successfully used in different applications, e.g., for blocker search in soft shadow rendering [SS07]. When used for occlusion culling, n-buffers require significantly less depth comparisons than conventional occlusion query based approaches. However, n-buffer queries are still slower than conventional occlusion queries on current GPUs, and considerably more conservative.

Geometric from-point algorithms Recently there has been renewed interest in this kind of algorithms, with applications mainly in computing the propagation of sound, where any sampling error due to the insufficient resolution of an image space algorithm leads to disturbing artifacts. As occluder fusion is difficult in object space, the algorithm of Chandak et al. [CATM09] subdivides the view frustra of the point light sources and adjusts the far plane of the sub-frustra if they are blocked by a *single* strong occluder. The

2.4. Visibility culling

blocker is computed using simple and efficient intersection tests in Plücker space.

The algorithm is significantly faster than previous geometric algorithms, and the authors state that their method is superior to image-based approaches in the context of sound rendering because of the greater accuracy and guaranteed error bounds, and that rasterization requires up to 32 x 32K resolution to achieve acceptable quality in scenes like the Powerplant. On the downside, the algorithm is still slower than methods based on rasterization. Furthermore, it is unclear how conservative the algorithm is, as concave occluders are not identified as blocker in order to keep the computations fast and simple. Hence it is a question if such an algorithm can be useful for online occlusion culling in the future, considering the fact that conservativity is not a requirement for online occlusion culling algorithms. For online occlusion culling, image-space algorithm using hardware occlusion queries have the advantage that they naturally sample the image space in exactly the necessary granularity.

2.4.3.1 Algorithms using hardware occlusion queries

Hardware support An OpenGL extension for occlusion queries was first suggested by Bartz et al. [BMH98]. Such an occlusion query returns the number of visible pixels of the primitives sent between a start and end tag, without requiring any readback. The first attempt for a hardware implementation came with the `HP_occlusion_test` extension, which was still pretty useless in retrospect, because it was slow and involved long waiting times for the query to finish. Later `NV_occlusion_query` was introduced which subsequently evolved into the official `ARB_occlusion_query` extension [cor]. It has the important functionality to test if a query result is available, which is essential to avoid idle time in the CPU when waiting for the query to return.

There is a relatively new extension called `NV_conditional_render` which renders geometry conditionally based on the result of an occlusion query without intervention of the CPU. It has an additional parameter that determines if the hardware should be forced to wait for the query to finish before ren-

Chapter 2. Related Work

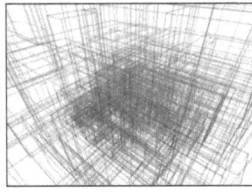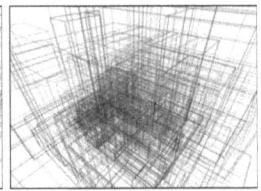

Figure 2.16: In this visualization of a view in the Powerplant (left), the green nodes correspond to successful queries, the red nodes to wasted queries, while no query has been issued for the blue nodes. On a NVidia Geforce5900 GPU, the original CHC algorithm (middle) wastes many queries, while the NOHC algorithm (right) can avoid most of the overhead. Image courtesy of Guthe et al. [GBK06].

dering or not [cor]. However, to our knowledge there is no scientific paper that explicitly uses this quite elegant functionality up to now.

Before dedicated hardware support for occlusion queries existed, online occlusion culling was mostly considered too costly for practical use, with some notable exceptions like the software based dPVS system from Aila et al. [AM04]. Only after the introduction of hardware accelerated occlusion queries, the potential of online occlusion culling gained the attention of both the research community and the industry, and opened the field for a variety of algorithms [KS01, HSLM02, GSYM03, SBS04, KS05]. However, the queries still come with a non-negligible cost, and algorithms have to find a way to use the latency until the result returns in a meaningful way. A naive hierarchical implementation which waits for the query result at each node before further traversing a hierarchy can actually *slow down* rendering significantly due to the idle time of GPU and CPU – this is where temporal coherence comes into play.

Temporal coherence The *Coherent Hierarchical Culling* (CHC) [BWPP04] algorithm utilizes *temporal coherence* to avoid the idle time. The CHC algorithm traverses nodes in a front-to-back order. Nodes that were visible in the last frame are still assumed visible in the current frame and vice-versa. Hence we always wait for the query result of a previously invisible node. Likewise,

2.4. Visibility culling

previously visible nodes are always rendered in the current frame. In the original CHC algorithm a query is always issued for previously visible nodes, but we do not wait for the result. Only when the query returns and the result is available we use it for the visibility classification in the next frame. For this purpose the pending queries are managed in a dedicated query queue. Fortunately, graphics hardware provides a cheap way to test if a query result is available. This way, both CPU and GPU are kept busy while waiting for query results. One major drawback of this algorithm is that too many queries for previously visible nodes are issued. Therefore the authors suggested to test previously visible nodes only every number of frames.

As can be seen in Figure 2.16), a problem of the original CHC algorithm is the high number of wasted occlusion queries (i.e., queries that report an object to be visible or queries that are more costly than rendering the node itself), which induce an significant overhead and make CHC clearly slower than view-frustum culling for view points where most of the scene is visible. The *Near Optimal Hierarchical Culling* (NOHC) [GBK06] algorithm computes the probability that a node will stay visible based on a statistical model of the estimated screen coverage due to objects rendered previously in the current frame. The expected value for accumulated screen coverage c_{scr} after $i+1$ rendered objects is computed as

$$c_{scr}(O_{i+1}) = c_{scr}(O_i) + (1 - c_{scr}(O_i))c(O_i), \tag{2.7}$$

where $C(O_i)$ is the estimated screen coverage of object O_i. The feasibility of a query is then decided using a sophisticated cost model that takes the probability that a node is still visible into account, and weights it with the cost of a query versus the cost of rendering an object. These quantities are measured during an offline hardware calibration step that samples different parameters like time required for rasterization or time required for transformation. Note that, this calibration model still does not take the complex interaction of queries and objects during rendering into account, and the fact that much of the overhead of a query is caused by state changes that happen during this interaction.

Chapter 2. Related Work

Algorithms like CHC or NOHC induce a radical change of the inner loop of any rendering engine, and a fast and robust integration into an existing engine is usually not trivial. Most modern rendering engines aim to minimize the state changes – first the visible objects are collected in some sort of render queue, then their patches (i.e., entities consisting of the same material) are sorted by material, and at last the content of the render queue is rendered at once using a single API call.

Instead, these algorithms require an approximate front-to-back rendering, and interleave rendering and querying to reduce the query latency. This constraint imposes a completely different ordering of renderable objects and prevents effective material sorting. One possibility is to impose a depth pass before the actual rendering pass. Depending on the hardware, this two-pass approach could be slower than one-pass rendering. Furthermore, the interleaving requires one API rendering call per rendered node of the hierarchy. This is not the intended usage, thus potentially causing a huge software overhead, especially for scenes with many visible nodes. It is therefore highly scene dependent if the benefit of occlusion culling outweighs the cost, which is a situation that seriously reduces the value of the occlusion culling algorithm, and will be addressed by our new improved algorithm in Chapter 4.

2.4.4 Hybrid rendering systems

In the following we describe methods that combine visibility culling with other real-time rendering techniques like IBR or LODs in an interesting, non-trivial way.

2.4.4.1 Massive model visualization

Very complex scenes cannot be handled by visibility alone. Some systems combine visibility culling with an image-based or polygonal simplification of the model representation. Dealing with highly complex scenes additionally requires some kind of out-of-core prefetching mechanism.

One of these systems is the well-known GigaWalk system [BSGM02]. Using a combination of conservative occlusion culling, either traditional or hi-

2.4. Visibility culling

Figure 2.17: DoubleEagle tanker with 82M triangles rendered with the GigaWalk system on an SGI station with 3 300 MHZ CPUS and 2 IR2 GPUS. Image courtesy of Baxter et al. [BSGM02].

erarchical LODs, load balancing between both CPUs and GPUs, and a novel object clustering scheme, this system managed to render complex environments like the Powerplant or the DoubleEagle Tanker shown in Figure 2.17 at real time frame rates back in the year 2002. However, it requires significant preprocessing times to establish the object hierarchy and to compute the LODs.

Gobetti et al. [GM05] presented a system for out-of-core rendering of very large data sets at interactive rates. During preprocessing, they generate a coarse binary space partition of the triangle soup. The inner nodes contain a volumetric representation consisting of a number of cubical voxels, which are visibility-aware volumetric approximations of the particular part of the scene when viewed from a distance. The approximations are created by sampling the full resolution dataset. During runtime, the system applies online culling with hardware occlusion queries. For distant parts of the scene it renders the volumetric approximations of the geometry together with a dedicated parametric vertex program.

Another system for visualizing large data sets was proposed by Brüderlin et al. [BHP07]. Independent of Bittner et al. [BWPP04], they invented an algorithm that uses temporal coherence and interleaves rendering and querying. For geometry that is sufficiently far away they simply switch to point-based rendering. This simple but powerful system can render many instances of the Boeing model with billions of triangles in interactive time.

Chapter 2. Related Work

2.4.4.2 Visibility-based simplifications

Recently a number of algorithms were proposed that use visibility properties to choose a proper LOD representation or image-based representation.

Andujar et al. introduced the concept of Hardly Visible Sets [CAB00] (HVS). They propose two metrics describing the *perceptual degree* of visibility of an object, one based on absolute accumulated size of the visible regions, one based on the maximal size of connected visible regions. These metrics controls the used LOD level. Although no user study is given, the second metric seems to be more useful, because of the greater perceptiveness of the human visual system to errors in connected regions.

Drettakis et al. [DBD*07] proposed an algorithm that controls level of detail based on perception. The methods takes *masking* into account when choosing the LOD level, utilizing the fact that high frequencies caused by e.g., foliage, or high contrast shadows, will prevent the user to perceive the differences between the original geometry and the simplified geometry. According to their user study, the result of their pipeline is consistent with what users perceive. However, the computations of the so called *threshold maps* impose a huge overhead (by definition they require to render the original model as a comparison), which makes the algorithm infeasible for most real-time applications.

Charalambos et al. [CBWR07] modified the CHC algorithm [BWPP04] for efficiently choosing the appropriate HLOD [EMWVB01] level based on the visibility of the node. Their metric just takes the number of visible pixels into account, hence important visual properties like the connectivity of the visible pixels cannot be evaluated.

2.4.4.3 Complex vegetation scenes

A challenging class of scenes for any rendering system are large vegetation scenes, like forests. Using only binary visibility for extremely complex foliage scenes is difficult because of two reasons, 1) the complex, mostly unconnected geometry is a nightmare for most visibility methods, including sampling-based methods, 2) many trees are still visible only through small holes. The

2.5. Visibility computations for realistic lighting

Figure 2.18: Visualization of a forest scene using the method of Erez et al. The red areas correspond to the visible parts of the impostors. Image courtesy of Erez et al. [SLCO*04]).

survey of Mantler et al. [MTF03] shows that many methods for rendering large vegetation scenes use non-polygonal representations for the trees like billboards or volume textures [DN04]. The method of Erez et al. [SLCO*04] exploits the property that many trees can be seen only through small holes for visibility-based simplification. They test the visibility of the trees against an occlusion buffer using occlusion queries. If a tree is tested to be visible, a slight overestimation of the tree is used to update the occlusion buffer, while the tree is rendered in full geometry. The trees that are tested to be invisible in the occlusion buffer are classified as background and rendered with impostors. The impostors can only be visible through small holes due to the slight overestimation of occluders, hence the typical parallax error of impostors is almost not noticeable. Figure 2.18 shows that the visible parts of the background are consists mostly of unconnected image noise, hence filling them up with impostors is sufficient. In a real forest scene, most trees and trunks can be considered as background, and the savings can be significant.

2.5 Visibility computations for realistic lighting

The biggest bottle neck to in order to achieve realistic lighting in real time is to solve the visibility queries fast enough. In this section we investigate different categories of algorithms that compute realistic lighting effects, and focus

Chapter 2. Related Work

on their handling of complex visibility interactions. First we discuss shadow algorithms for direct illumination, then global illumination algorithms, and at last ambient occlusion algorithms, which yields a relatively cheap approximation of the appearance of full-fledged global illumination.

2.5.1 Shadow algorithms

Direct illumination produces either hard shadows in case of a point or directional light source, or soft shadows in case of an area light source. The problem areas of shadow computation have a direct relationship to the problem areas of visibility culling. This becomes apparent when comparing the terminology of these two fields. E.g., in from-region visibility for visibility preprocessing we speak of the penumbra of an object as induced by a view cell, while hard shadow maps can be resolved with a single from-point visibility query. A huge body of papers have been proposed that cover hard shadows for real-time rendering, which fall either into the category of shadow mapping [Wil78] or shadow volumes [Cro77]. While shadow volumes are the more accurate technique, shadow maps received more attention in recent years because of their greater efficiency and flexibility (they also work for alpha-mapped and bump-mapped geometry), and they are also extensively used in real time global illumination algorithms. The biggest issue of hard shadow maps are aliasing effects due to the discretization process, which can be separated into perspective error and projection error. Most recent papers deal with reducing aliasing to improve the shadow quality. Perspective shadow mapping techniques [LGQ*08, WSP04] greatly improve the visual quality compared to uniform shadow maps by distributing the shadow map resolution better. As a single shadow map does not give sufficient resolution in all cases, various techniques have been introduced that aim to improve shadow quality with multiple shadow maps, using either view-frustum slicing [ZSXL06], or automatic shadow partitioning with an error threshold [FFBG01, GW07]. Other methods reduce anti-aliasing by filtering the results of the shadow tests using percentage closer filtering [RSC87] or by pre-filtering the shadow maps [DL06, AMB*07].

2.5. Visibility computations for realistic lighting

Another huge body of work has been dedicated to the rendering of soft shadow. A slightly outdated survey of soft shadow algorithms was proposed by Hasenfratz et al. [HLHS03], which still delivers a good overview of algorithms based on both shadow maps or shadow volumes, and provides a useful classification of soft shadow methods according to their properties, from slow and physically based to plausible and fast. Fernando proposed a cheap and robust technique that approximates soft shadows with a variable sized percentage closer filter kernel [Fer05]. Many of the recently developed soft shadow algorithms are based on backprojection [GBP06, GBP07, SS07, BCS08]. These methods are GPU friendly, as they use a single shadow map to represent a discrete approximation of the occluders between shaded point and light source. To evaluate the percentage of the light source that is blocked, these methods search for occluders in the shadow map and backproject them onto the source. For small light sources they achieve almost correct shadows, while large light sources with big penumbrae negatively influence performance and cause visual artifacts. Physically correct shadows in dynamic scenes with arbitrarily shaped dynamic light sources are still not feasible in real time.

2.5.2 Real-time global illumination

Convincing real-time dynamic global illumination with both diffuse and glossy materials is one of the major goals left in 3D computer graphics research. The bottle neck lies in the required number of visibility queries – it is necessary to have hundreds or thousands of queries per frame in order to compute convincing global illumination. Recently a lot of progress has been made, and novel GPU-friendly approaches [RGK*08, DSDD07] demonstrate that very subtle soft shadow and colour bleeding effects are possible in interactive to real-time frame rates (refer to Figure 2.19). In the following we investigate how various methods aim to approximate the rendering equation 1.3.1, and focus on their way to resolve the visibility interactions.

Precomputed radiance transfer (PRT) [SKS02] allows dynamic per-vertex relighting for static scenes lit from an environment map. The method makes

Chapter 2. Related Work

Figure 2.19: Methods like implicit visibility and antiradiance [DSDD07] compute subtle global illumination effects (color bleeding, soft contact shadows) in interactive time or real time (Image courtesy of Dachsbacher et al. [DSDD07]).

use of the property that the outgoing radiance computation can be separated into incident light and a transfer function (i.e., the cosine weighted visibility function over the hemisphere), which maps the incident light to outgoing radiance and can be precomputed. By projecting both source radiance as well as transfer function into the *spherical harmonics basis*, the outgoing radiance can be evaluated on the GPU with a simple vector dot product between coefficient vectors. Also, the visibility functions can be compressed to reasonable data sizes. The work of Sloan et al. [SKS02] spawned a long list of follow up papers. Some investigate the usage of different basis functions like *nonlinear wavelets [NRH03]*, which allow higher frequency shadows but are more difficult to evaluate. Lehtinen et al. [Leh07] present a general framework for developing finite-element methods that can use precomputed light transport. On the downside, PRT methods have considerable preprocessing and storage cost, and only low frequency lighting can be computed efficiently in real time. In the rest of this survey, we concentrate on more dynamic methods that require less preprocessing, which we believe to be the future direction for real-time global illumination.

2.5. Visibility computations for realistic lighting

Many of the following methods use a deferred shading pipeline [ST90, Shi05]. A deferred shading pipeline stores pixel properties like colors, normals, depth, or positions in separate buffers, called *G-buffers*, and uses them to compute the final shading in a separate screen-space step. The advantage of deferred shading lies in the fact that the shading complexity can be decoupled from the scene complexity. As the performance depends mostly on the size of the used render target, it is a common practice to compute the low frequency indirect illumination separately in a lower resolution render target and upsample it later on.

Dachsbacher and Stamminger [DS05] use only a single *reflective shadow map* from the light source to capture the surfaces that cause indirect illumination, making the crude simplification to completely ignoring visibility between indirect light source and receiver pixel for the sake of performance. Each texel in the shadow map is treated as a diffuse light source, storing flux information as well as surface normal. In a screen space pass the method computes the incident indirect illumination at each pixel by gathering the nearest pixel lights in the shadow map, and weighting their contribution to the illumination with the squared distance to the currently shaded pixel. Later Dachsbacher and Stamminger [DS06] developed an improved version of this algorithm, which uses importance sampling to select a subset of point lights on the shadow map, and distributes their indirect illumination by splatting variably shaped kernels. To limit the fill rate during accumulation of the light contribution, they fit the size and shape of the kernels to match the power and the shape of the light sources. Both methods using reflective shadow maps achieve real time frame rates for standard game scenes. The splatting approach is faster and can handle caustics quite well. However, both methods are prone to flickering artifacts and drastically simplify global illumination by ignoring visibility.

Instant radiosity [Kel97] is a technique that is well suited for global illumination on the GPU. This method shoots random light paths from the light source, and creates *virtual light sources* (VPLs) at the intersections with geometry to simulate the indirect light bounces. In comparison to reflective shadow maps, instant radiosity takes visibility into ac-

Chapter 2. Related Work

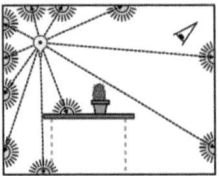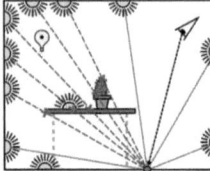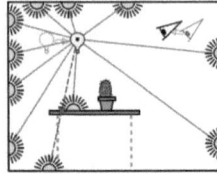

Figure 2.20: (left) Instant Radiosity shoots paths from the light source, and creates virtual point lights at the intersection with geometry. (middle) Using shadow maps, the visibility of each VPL and their contribution to the current image is determined. (right) Temporal coherence: When the view point or light source moves, only one of the VPLs becomes invisible and has to be invalidated, while all the others can be reused. Image courtesy of Laine et al. [LSK*07].

count by determining the contribution of each VPL to the current view with paraboloid shadow maps (as can be seen in Figure 2.20), which allows fast visibility queries on the GPU. Because of its GPU-friendliness the algorithm became very popular, and several variations of the original algorithm have been proposed since, which all reach interactive to real-time frame rates [SIP06, SIP07, LSK*07, RGK*08].

The performance of these algorithms can be significantly improved with *interleaved sampling [KH01, SIMP06]*. The original idea was to create irregular sampling patterns out of several interleaved hardware-friendly regular patterns [KH01]. The technique can be used to interleave VPL computations, and assign a separate set of VPLs to each sub-buffer, exploiting the fact that it is sufficient to compute low frequency indirect illumination in lower resolution without noticeable loss of quality. Hence a number of lower resolution images of the scene are rendered into sub-buffers, each with a small offset. In case that the offsets are regular, we obtain nxm regular sampling patterns for each pixel of the output image, where each pixel within such a pattern has a different set of VPLs. Segovia et al. [SIMP06] propose a two-pass algorithm to efficiently compute these interleaved sampling patterns in a deferred shading pipeline. In the first step they rearrange the full sized image into the nxm sub-buffers by using divisions and modulo operations. Now there

2.5. Visibility computations for realistic lighting

Figure 2.21: (left) Imperfect shadow maps use a coarse point based representation of the scene (pink and yellow VPLs use only the pink and yellow points, respectively). (right) Imperfect shadow maps generated in a single frame. (top) With and (bottom) without push-pull algorithm for repairing the holes. Image courtesy of Ritschel et al. [RGK*08].

is coherent access to all pixels that use the same VPLs, and the method can efficiently perform the shading computations on each of these sub-buffers in parallel. Afterwards the method gathers the shaded pixels again with the reverse operation, and computes the output pixels using a discontinuity buffer and a Gaussian blur filter.

Laine et al. [LSK*07] exploit temporal coherence to reach real-time frame rates in a variation of the Instant Radiosity algorithm. For the sake of performance, the authors restrict their method to compute first bounce indirect illumination, stating that the first bounce is sufficient for plausible global illumination. The method queries the validity of the VPLs using a ray caster, and recomputes only a budget of invalid shadow maps in a frame while keeping the others unchanged (refer to Figure 2.20). The algorithm uses a 2D Delaunay triangulation to manage the VPL distribution. The main task of the algorithm is to keep a good distribution of VPLs in every frame. When choosing the location of new VPLs, they minimize *dispersion*, which is computed as the radius of the largest empty circle that contains no sample points. The exploitation of temporal coherence comes with the prize that changes in the scene are captured with a certain latency, and shadows cast from dynamic objects are not supported.

Chapter 2. Related Work

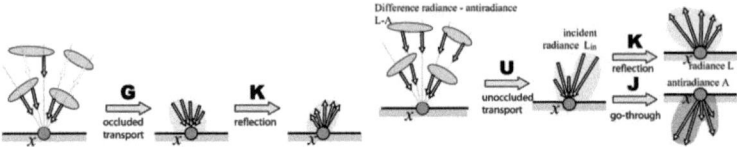

Figure 2.22: (a) Conventional light transport (b) Reformulation without geometric term G that computes explicit visibility, using antiradiance A (negative light) to compensate superfluous light due to missing occlusion. Image courtesy of Dachsbacher et al. [DSDD07].

A big step into the direction of fully dynamic real time global illumination was the realization that it is not necessary to compute high-resolution shadow maps for capturing the mostly low frequency indirect illumination [RGK*08]. Instead, a low resolution point representation is used to capture visibility in the scene, which can be quickly rendered into the shadow maps in this variant of the Instant Radiosity algorithm, denoted as *imperfect shadow maps* (refer to Figure 2.21). Artifacts in the form of holes in the shadow maps are closed with a push-pull algorithm. Imperfect shadow maps allow computing hundreds of shadow maps at interactive frame rates.

As visibility queries are the most expensive part of global illumination, Dachsbacher et al. [DSDD07] reformulate the rendering equation to completely avoid explicit computation of visibility. Instead, they developed a recursive formula that converges towards the correct lighting solution using the notion of negative light, denoted as *antiradiance*. As depicted in Figure 2.22, the rendering equation can be written in terms of linear operators

$$L(p,\omega') = E(p,\omega') + (KGL)(p,\omega') \qquad (2.8)$$

where E is the self emmision, K is the reflection operator, and G is the geometry operator which computes explicit visibility to find the first surface in direction ω'. In a number of steps, they reformulate it into the recursive formula

2.5. Visibility computations for realistic lighting

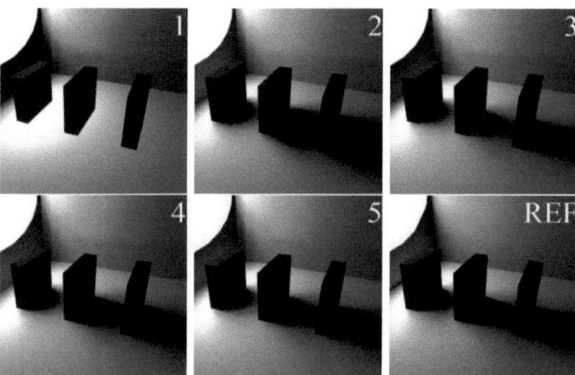

Figure 2.23: 1-5: The algorithm of Dachsbacher et al. alternately adds (1, 3, 5) and subtracts (so called antiradiance, 2 and 4) light until convergence to an acceptable solution (5). (REF) Path tracing reference. Image courtesy of Dachsbacher et al. [DSDD07].

$$L = E + KU(L - A)$$
$$A = JU(L - A),$$

where A is the antiradiance, U denotes an unoccluded transport operator that replaces G, and J is a simple go-through operator, which transmits light through surfaces as if they where transparent. Note that, instead of radiance L, the recursive formula propagates the difference of radiance to antiradiance $(L - A)$. Figure 2.23 shows the basic idea of implicit visibility: First the scene is lit without considering occlusion (image 1). Later on the superfluous radiance is subtracted, using antiradiance (image 2). Now radiance is underestimated and must be added again (image 3), and so on, and so forth (images 4 and 5).

The highly optimized GPU implementation is similar to traditional radiosity [GTGB84], but they also have to discretisise the directional components of individual patches to distribute the antiradiance, which in return

Chapter 2. Related Work

Figure 2.24: Stanford dragon rendered with the screen-space ambient occlusion method of Fox and Compton [FC08].

also allows them to render glossy BRDFs. For all shown scenarios the method is faster than traditional path tracing and does not display the typical image noise of path tracing algorithms (REF method in Figure 2.23). While the image quality is convincing, the high memory requirements restrict the method to small and medium sized scenes like the oriental room shown in Figure 2.19.

2.5.3 Ambient occlusion

Global illumination techniques are still rarely used in games or other real time applications. *Ambient occlusion* (AO), on the other hand, is extensively used in areas like production rendering [Lan02, PG04], because it is a relatively simple and cheap shading technique, and it greatly enhances the appearance of a scene with soft contact and self shadows, requiring no additional lighting, as can be seen in Figure 2.24. Ambient occlusion, introduced by Zhukov et al. [ZIK98], measures the reverse surface exposure. Assuming a perfectly diffuse material and a perfectly ambient lighting situation, ambient occlusion strips down the lighting computation to pure integration of the visibility function over the hemisphere, as can be seen in Equation 1.3.2. It describes the percentage of incident ambient light on a surface point that is occluded by surrounding geometry (i.e., it corresponds to quantitative from-point visibility), and is used for shading by modulating the ambient color of

2.5. Visibility computations for realistic lighting

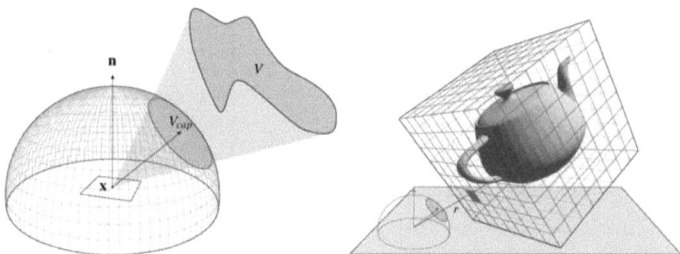

Figure 2.25: Ambient occlusion field of an object. (left) Spherical cap approximation of the occluded hemisphere due to an object. (right) The method stores the spherical cap an occluder subtends for a given direction as radial function parametrized by distance r in a cube map centered at the object. Image courtesy of Kontkanen et al. [KL05].

the surface point with it. Thus ambient occlusion is per definition a perfect example for the computation of qualitative visibility from a point and its application. From a physical point of view, ambient occlusion could be seen as the diffuse illumination due to the sky [Lan02].

A byproduct of ambient occlusion is the so called *bent normal*, which is the average direction of arriving light [Lan02]. It is computed by averaging over all unoccluded directions. Using the bent normal instead of the actual normal for illumination and environment lookups gives a more realistic appearance.

We will first discuss methods that operate in object space, and then methods that operate in image space, which are also known as screen-space ambient occlusion.

2.5.3.1 Object space methods

In recent years several conceptually different approaches have been proposed that make the online calculation of ambient occlusion in dynamic scenes feasible for real-time applications. Some *object space* approaches exist that accumulate ambient occlusion by distributing the *occlusion power* of each occluder to all the other objects in the range of interest [KL05, MMAH07].

The algorithm of Kontkanen et al. precomputes *ambient occlusion fields*

Chapter 2. Related Work

for each object. More specifically, for each position in a field surrounding the occluding object, it precomputes the spherical cap subtended by the occluder as approximation of the occluder. The spherical cap is determined by an average occlusion direction and a solid angle. To keep the memory requirements low, the method stores this information as a radial function of the distance r in a 2D cube map accessed with the direction. After computing the spherical cap, the ambient occlusion integral can be efficiently evaluated. Figure 2.25 shows the spherical cap approximation on the left, and the ambient occlusion field lookup using the direction vector on the right.

The authors suggest two implementations, one loops over all occluders for each receiver object to accumulate the occlusion, while the second implementation uses a deferred shading pipeline to loop over all occluders for all receiver pixels. Clearly, the second implementation has the better runtime behavior of $O(n)$ in the number of objects, while the first variant has $O(n^2)$. Malmer et al. [MMAH07] proposed the same idea as parallel work, but store the occlusion information as scalar values in a 3D texture instead. The method can be extended to compute diffuse color bleeding. Both methods have problems to handle overlapping occluders correctly. Kontkanen et al. suggest to use multiplicative blending, while Malmer et al. propose the fusion of two spherical caps into a single larger one.

Conceptually similar methods were proposed for the computation of soft shadows [ZHL*05, RWS*06, SGNS07], which can also be extended to compute indirect illumination [GJW08]. Zhou et al. [ZHL*05] precompute the occlusion power of rigid objects on receiver points in so called *object occlusion fields* and project it into the spherical harmonics basis. Likewise, light sources are stored as *source radiance fields*, and the authors refer to both as *shadow fields*. The radiance on any given receiver point can be calculated as combination of such shadow fields. As these shadow fields are independent of the position in the scene, the algorithm is able to handle soft shadows cast by moving objects, illuminated from large environmental and local light sources. The method accumulates blocker visibility by calculating the product of occlusion fields O_i:

2.5. Visibility computations for realistic lighting

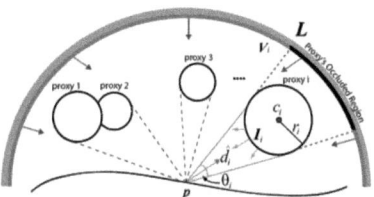

Figure 2.26: The occlusion of blocker objects can approximated by accumulating the SH visibility vectors of spherical proxies at each receiver point. Sloan et al. also account for inter-reflections I. Image courtesy of Sloan et al. [SGNS07].

$$O_p = \prod_{i=1}^{n} O_i \qquad (2.9)$$

where O_p denotes the combined occlusion, and O_i is the spherical harmonics projection of the visibility function that is 0 if a direction is blocked by object i, 1 otherwise. Note that, unlike the related ambient occlusion methods [KL05, MMAH07], this method can account for approximate blocker accumulation, as spherical harmonics give a low frequency notion of direction. The method is computationally expensive, because the spherical harmonics product and rotation are very costly, and feasible only for a couple of objects. For low frequency shadows, the authors report real-time frame rates. Using a wavelet basis, they can handle all-frequency shadows at interactive frame rates.

Ren et al. [RWS*06] avoid precomputation of the shadow fields completely and support deformable geometry by approximating the geometry with proxy spheres. Computing the (reverse) visibility function V_i induced by blocker i from point p (as shown in Figure 2.26) simplifies to

$$V_i(\omega') = \begin{cases} 1, & \text{if } \omega' \cdot \vec{d} \geq \cos(\theta_i) \\ 0, & \text{otherwise.} \end{cases} \qquad (2.10)$$

Occlusion O_i of the visibility vector i is

Chapter 2. Related Work

$$O_i = 1 - V_i = (\sqrt{4\pi}, 0, .., 0) - V_i, \tag{2.11}$$

where the SH vector 1 denotes the constant 1 over a sphere, which has only 1 non-zero component. Their second contribution enormously accelerates blocker accumulation by using a standard engineer's trick: They exchange the costly spherical harmonics product with a sum of log visibility vectors O_i, using the fact that

$$\prod_{i=1}^{n} 0_i \approx \exp \sum_{i=1}^{n} \log 0_i, \tag{2.12}$$

which enables them to move the entire computation onto the GPU. Finally they obtain the correct result using spherical harmonics exponentiation. In order to reduce complexity, they organize the blockers in a hierarchy and choose the hierarchy level based on distance.

Sloan et al. [SGNS07] move the computation of blocker accumulation with log visibility vectors into image space by splatting sphere proxies on the receiver pixels, which gives them a large speedup compared to previous per-vertex approaches. As can be seen in Figure 2.26, they also account for inter-reflections between objects by accumulating unshaded radiance from the illumination due to the environment map. It is sufficient to compute the low frequency indirect illumination in smaller resolutions and use bilateral upsampling [ED04, BSD08] to combine it with the final image. On a GeForce 8800, they achieve real time frame rates in low resolutions of maximal 256x256 for scenes with about 6000 vertices.

Bunnell [Bun05] proposed an interesting per-vertex ambient occlusion method for dynamic scenes. It is a finite element method with resemblance to hierarchical radiosity, but is much faster because it avoids explicit visibility queries. Also, it accounts for approximate occluder overlap, unlike many other ambient occlusion algorithms [KL05, MMAH07] using a multipass approach.

The method assumes geometry to consist of spherical elements that are centered around the vertices, with a normal and an area, that is approximately 1/3 the area of the triangles incident to the vertex. The front faces

2.5. Visibility computations for realistic lighting

emit and reflect light, while the back faces transmit light and cast shadows. For every element, the algorithm computes how much solid angle of the hemisphere is occluded by all the other elements, using the following form factor for the influence of emitter element E on receiver element R:

$$1 - \frac{r cos(\theta_E) \max(1, 4cos(\theta_R))}{\sqrt{\frac{A_E}{\pi} + d^2}}. \tag{2.13}$$

In this formula θ_E and θ_R are the angles between emitter surface and receiver surface and transmittance direction, respectively, d is the distance between R and E, and A_E the emitter area. After the first pass, there is overshadowing because occluder overlap was not taken into account yet. In the second pass, the same calculations are repeated, but overlap is accounted for by multiplying the shadowing term of an emitter with its own accessibility from the first pass, based on the assumption that elements that are in shadow contribute less to the shadowing itself. More passes will account for triple shadowed surfaces or more. To break down the quadratic complexity in the number of vertices, Bunnell uses hierarchical level of detail based on the distance to the receiver elements, which reduces the complexity to $O(n \log(n))$. It is straightforward to extend the algorithm to compute diffuse color bleeding. The author also suggests to estimate the bent normal by weighting the normalized transmittance direction with the form factor and subtracting it from the actual surface normal. Similar ideas have been later used by Dachsbacher et al. [DSDD07] in their antiradiance algorithm, e.g., the convergence towards the proper lighting solution. However, the algorithm of Dachsbacher et al. is based on a rigorous mathematical concept that results in a novel reformulation of the rendering equation, while the method of Bunnell is a more practical approach that uses many ad hoc assumptions.

2.5.3.2 Image-space methods

Image-space ambient occlusion methods, often referred to as screen space ambient occlusion (SSAO) [Mit07], interpret the frame buffer as a discrete scene approximation. Screen-space algorithms have the benefit of a constant overhead that does not depend on the scene complexity. This output-sensitivity

Chapter 2. Related Work

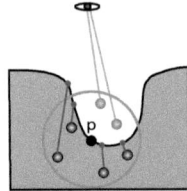

Figure 2.27: The SSAO method of Mittring et al. [Mit07] uses a spherical sampling kernel and a depth test to determine if a sample is occluded. In this case, 4 out of 6 samples are occluded. Originally the samples are unweighted, in later implementations they are correctly cosine weighted.

and its good performance makes SSAO is a very useful technique, hence we worked on improving SSAO ourselves, and discuss our work in Chapter 5. The beneficial properties of SSAO come with the price that certain information about the scene is lost in the process. Therefore SSAO methods have problems on the borders of the screen, and with surfaces that are not represented in the depth buffer. The issues can only be compensated with additional computational effort - the first problem by using G-buffers that are larger than the actually displayed window, the second problem by using depth peeling to capture additional surfaces, and by moving the camera backwards by a certain offset to capture surfaces that are behind the view point.

SSAO has a lot of practical relevance: The first SSAO implementation by Mittring [Mit07] came to use in the game Crysis, and up to this date many high profile games like Starcraft 2 use SSAO to increase realism. As can be seen in Figure 2.27, the method of Mittring uses a spherical sampling kernel that is centered around the current pixel, and makes a depth comparison in order to estimate the number of samples that are occluded. The original implementation did not yet take the incident angle into account, hence samples that fell into the lower hemisphere of the surface also counted. This problem can be compensated by assuming pixels to be unshadowed if less than half of the samples are occluded. The banding artifacts that occur for a reasonable number of 8-32 samples are traded for less distracting noise, by reflecting the

2.5. Visibility computations for realistic lighting

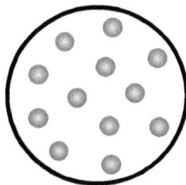 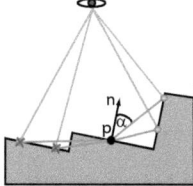

Figure 2.28: The methods of Fox and Compton [SA07] and Shanmugam et al. [SA07] use a 2D sampling kernel (left) that is projected into world space (right). The sample is weighted with the cosine of the angle α between surface normal and vector to the sample, and the distance. Samples below the hemisphere have no contribution.

sample positions around a per-pixel random normal vector. The quality of the method can be improved by using importance sampling to better distribute the samples (i.e., more samples are created close to the current pixel). In order to increase the samples that have an actual contribution because they are in the upper hemisphere of a surface point, the samples can be transformed to be always above the tangent plane of the surface. A number of conceptually related SSAO methods were proposed [SA07, FC08, BSD08, RGS09].

Shanmugam and Arikan [SA07] presented a two-stage image space method. The high-frequency near-field ambient occlusion is computed with a 2D sampling kernel that is projected into the world space. They treat each sample as spherical occluder with a certain size, and weight the sample contribution with the angle incident to the surface of the shaded pixel as well as the distance. Note that, unlike the method of Mittring [Mit07], this algorithm does not require a depth comparison of each sample. The second stage computes the low frequency far field ambient occlusion using splatting of spherical occluders, similar to the method of Dachsbacher and Stamminger [DS06].

Fox and Compton [FC08] proposed an SSAO shading technique that is very similar to the method of Shanmugam and Arikan [SA07], but lacks a physical explanation, and the parameters are artist controlled. As shown in Figure 5.11, the method is easy to adjust and gives very nice results by emphasizing creases, while the method of Mittring [Mit07] is more physically

Chapter 2. Related Work

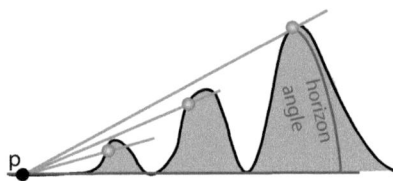

Figure 2.29: Using ray marching, horizon based ambient occlusion [BSD08] computes the horizon angle, which corresponds to the maximum angle of the hemisphere that is occluded by the horizon.

based and closer to the original ambient occlusion definition.

Horizon based ambient occlusion [BSD08] computes the percentage of the occluded hemisphere with an idea that is very similar to horizon mapping [Max88]. The method uses ray marching to find the maximum occluding angle between the image plane and the vector to the sample, in a fixed number of directions and sampling steps, as can be seen in Figure 2.29. The ambient occlusion is then computed as

$$AO = sin(h) - sin(t), \qquad (2.14)$$

where h is the horizon angle between image plane and sample direction, and t is the angle between image plane and the tangent plane induced by the normal at the current pixel. Note that, while all aforementioned SSAO methods have in common that they ignore all blockers between the sample and the shaded pixel for the sake of performance, this method iterates towards the correct solution depending on the number of ray marching steps.

Ritschel et al. [RGS09] extended their SSAO generation method to include directional information and first-bounce global illumination. The SSAO generation is almost identical to the original method of Mittring [Mit07], but also takes cosine and distance into account to accurately weight the samples that passed the depth test. When sampling the depth buffer to make the depth comparison, it is straightforward to also sample the color buffer and get indirect illumination almost for free. As can be seen in Figure 2.30), the

2.5. Visibility computations for realistic lighting

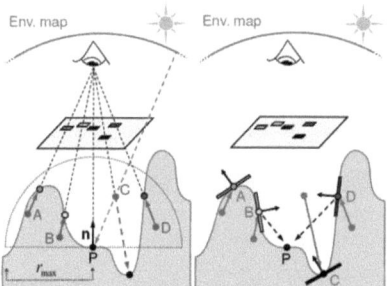

Figure 2.30: Screen-space indirect illumination [RGS09]: (left) First the visibility of the samples is determined (only sample C is visible). (right) Each visible sample is seen as a small oriented patch which emits the direct light stored in the color buffer towards shaded point P. Image courtesy of Ritschel et al. [RGS09].

method assumes each visible sample to be a small sender patch lit by direct illumination from the environment map. The influence of a sender patch to the indirect lighting L_{ind} in a pixel P is related to form factors known from radiosity [GTGB84]:

$$L_{ind}(P) = \sum_{i=1}^{n} \frac{\rho}{\pi} L_{s_i}(1 - V(\omega_i)) \frac{A_s cos(\theta_{s_i}) cos(\theta_{r_i})}{d_i^2}, \qquad (2.15)$$

where L_{pix} is the illumination stored at sender s_i, $V(\omega_i)$ the visibility of the sender, A_s the area of the sender patch, θ_{s_i} and θ_{r_i} are the angles between transmittance direction and sender normal as well as receiver normal in P, respectively, and d_i the distance between sender and receiver. This method also supports depth peeling for reducing the error due to the screen-space approximation.

2.5.3.3 Animated characters

Ambient occlusion for character animation can be achieved by precomputing ambient occlusion for a couple of key poses and then interpolating between them [KA06, KA07], at considerable storage cost.

Chapter 2. Related Work

Figure 2.31: Due to temporal coherence, most pixel information from the previous frame can be reused in the current frame (shown in blue) and only minor parts have to be recomputed (shown in red). Image courtesy of Scherzer et al. [SJW07].

2.6 Reprojection techniques for temporal coherence

Temporal coherence is an important topic in this thesis – we use it to accelerate online occlusion culling, and to improve the quality of screen-space ambient occlusion in real time. Therefore we now shortly discuss the previous work on using temporal coherence to improve the performance and rendering quality of real-time rendering algorithms, and in particular on reprojection techniques. It is a very intuitive idea to exploit temporal coherence to accelerate interactive walkthroughs. Between two consecutive frames, the view point will changes only marginally during the course of a walkthrough, and the images stay mostly coherent. A clever algorithm can use this coherence to recompute only the parts of the image that changed since the previous frame. Changes are induced by disocclusions on the silhouettes of objects or in creases, or by a change of the illumination. Figure 2.31 shows that a considerable amount of pixels shown in blue can be reused for moderate camera movements.

For a long time algorithms that exploit temporal coherence were mostly used in offline rendering and ray tracing. Bishop et al. [BFMZ94] proposed to use frameless rendering instead of the traditional frame-by-frame approach for ray tracing. They update the pixels in a randomized manner, hence avoiding the effect of image tearing in single buffer displays and having to

2.6. Reprojection techniques for temporal coherence

update only a fraction of the samples. Dayal et al. [DWWL05] improved on this approach by adaptively using more samples in regions with high temporal gradients, i.e., with a high degree of change.

Havran et al. [HBS03] use temporal coherence to speed up ray tracing in interactive walkthroughs by avoiding the overhead of traversal whenever possible. They use reprojection of visible points from the previous frame in order to predict the object intersected by a ray in the current frame. Tawara et al. [TMD*04] reduce the cost of global illumination techniques like density estimation, by moving the computation into the temporal domain and distributing it over several frames.

A rasterizer requires a high amount of coherence, and it is not feasible to handle pixels individually like in frameless rendering. However, temporal coherence can be efficiently used by reprojecting the last frame into the current frame and associating those pixels from the previous frame with the image pixels from the current frame that represent the same world space position. The GPU-based technique was independently proposed by Scherzer et al. [SJW07] (referred to as temporal reprojection) who specifically use it to improve the quality of hard shadows, and Nehab et al. [NSL*07] for their multi-purpose *shading cache*. The technique lead to a couple of follow up papers [SALY*08, PSALY*08, YNS*09]. Reprojection methods were shown to be useful for a variety of applications, like shadow mapping, anti-aliasing, or even motion blur [Ros07]. Both Scherzer et al. [SJW07] and Nehab et al. [NSL*07] use exponential smoothing to blend the last frame with the new frame in the form

$$f_t = \tau s + (1 - \tau) f_{t-1}, \qquad (2.16)$$

where s is the value computed in the current frame, and τ the exponential weighting factor between 0 and 1. Scherzer et al. [SJW07] additionally weight a shadow lookup sample according to the distance to the real texel center, which gives them an estimate of the confidence in the correctness of the lookup result. To improve the image quality for static frames, Scherzer et al. evaluate different jittering schemes, among which the rotational scheme has

Chapter 2. Related Work

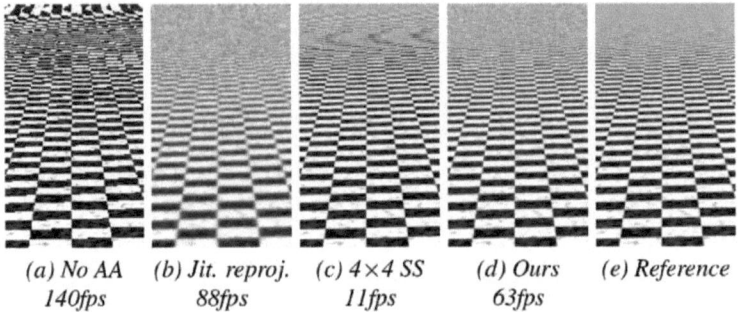

(a) No AA (b) Jit. reproj. (c) 4×4 SS (d) Ours (e) Reference
140fps   88fps   11fps   63fps

Figure 2.32: Reusing samples for many frames with reverse reprojection (for applications like anti-aliasing) causes blur artifacts. The image quality can be improved by sub-pixel sampling. From left to right: No super sampling, reprojection without subsampling, conventional super sampling, reprojection with subsampling, and a reference image showing the ground truth. Image courtesy of Yang et al. [YNS*09].

been reported to provide the best results.

All methods based on reprojection need a mechanism that determines when a sample point has become invalid and cannot be reused. In the simplest case, a single depth comparison between the reprojected sample and its stored counterpart from the previous frame can be used to detect disocclusions. In the terminology of the shading cache [NSL*07], we speak about cache hits and cache misses.

Sitthi-Amorn et al. [PSALY*08] attempt to generalize the shading cache approach and automatize it for pixel shader optimization. They identified the same parameters for all techniques that use reprojection for optimization: The cost of a pixel shader can be reduced for a single frame by spreading the computation over δn frames, denoted as the refresh period. As a tradeoff, using more frames induces a larger approximation error that is mainly caused by GPU-based bilinear resampling. In their cost-benefit model, they also consider the frequency and the penalty due to cache misses versus cache hits.

Yang et al. [YNS*09] use reprojection to improve supersampling both in

2.6. Reprojection techniques for temporal coherence

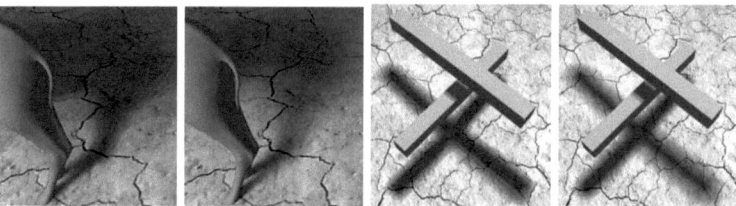

Figure 2.33: Reprojection used for fast multi-sample soft shadow rendering by rendering a single shadow map per frame from a random area light source sample and accumulating the results [SSMW09]. This method (images 2 and 4) can handle configurations that are problematic for single-sample methods like PCSS (images 1 and 4). Image courtesy of Scherzer et al. [SSMW09].

terms of speed and quality. They are the first to make a deeper analysis of the blur artifacts due to bilinear resampling. As a remedy, they fall back to use subsampling to increase the effective resolution. They succeed in reaching significantly faster frame rates than conventional super sampling with better quality, while avoiding most of the blurring artifacts associated with previous reprojection methods, as can bee seen in Figure 2.32. However, their analysis considers only a limited set of motions. Also, they do not take the orientation of the surfaces into account, which is an important factor judging from our experience, as steep surfaces can suffer from significant projection error and are prone to heavy blur artifacts.

Scherzer et al. [SSMW09] recently proposed using reprojection to quickly render multi-sample soft shadows. They evaluate a single new sample on the area light source per frame using a shadow map, and accumulate the results. In order to speed up convergence, they compute a first estimation of the real shadow using percentage-closer soft shadows (PCSS) [Fer05]. They also use a filter for blurring insufficiently converged shadows in the spatial domain. As can be seen in Figure 2.33 they achieve high-quality shadows for static scenes with a low overhead compared to hard shadow mapping. Unfortunately, their approach has problems with dynamic objects and moving light sources, which cause global changes in the illumination and reduce the potential of temporal coherence significantly.

Chapter 2. Related Work

In a GDC presentation, Smedberg et al. [SW09] proposed using reprojection to enhance the quality of SSAO independent from us. However, some details about the method are not publicly available, and they do not specifically address the proper invalidation of incorrect cache values, which is a key part of our approach in Chapter 5.

Imperfect shadow maps [RGK*08] allow hundreds of visibility queries per frame in interactive time. However, even such a large number of queries are insufficient to avoid typical undersampling artifacts, resulting in flickering between frames. Knecht [Kne09] combines the imperfect shadow mapping approach with temporal reprojection, removing most of these artifacts. Due to the low frequency nature of indirect illumination, the motion blur like artifacts caused by moving light sources and animated objects are not very distracting in the general case.

> We think too small, like the frog at the bottom of the well. He thinks the sky is only as big as the top of the well. If he surfaced, he would have an entirely different view.
>
> Mao Tse-Tung

3 Algorithms for Scene Preprocessing

In this chapter we discuss an important but often neglected problem - how to prepare a scene optimally for visibility computations. Most previous work dealt with the actual visibility computation algorithms. However, before this, the scene must be processed in a certain way. This requires solving a completely different set of problems, in particular the issue of creating a *good* set of view cells and objects (usually by means of subdivision). In this case, the meaning of "good" is an interesting question on its own. We show how to compute information about the visibility in the scene using global sampling, which is a common step in our algorithms. In the following sections, we propose two particular solutions to these problems. First we present an algorithm for view cell creation where the objects are assumed to be given. Then we tackle the much harder problem of optimizing a combined view space and object space subdivision. We show the dual relationship of view and object space, and that properties like memory cost and render cost depend on the interaction of both spaces.

3.1 Introduction

Traditional visibility preprocessing algorithms assume that a *view space* is partitioned into a set of *view cells* and the *object space* is partitioned into a

Chapter 3. Algorithms for Scene Preprocessing

set of *objects*. While there is a huge body of literature on how to calculate a PVS for a given view cell, the problem of how to actually define the view cells and objects has received only marginal attention so far.

A common scenario is that the partition of objects is already given (e.g, in a game studio where objects are specified manually in the modeling phase), and the task is to construct meaningful view cells. Note that a careful design of the view cells is crucial for several reasons: (1) view cells that take the visibility structure of the scene into account allow achieving smaller PVSs, and therefore faster rendering speed at runtime, (2) a bad view cell definition can severely impact the time required for the preprocessing step, and (3) the amount of memory required to store the PVS data depends strongly on the quality of the view cell distribution.

Consider, for example, a model of a city with buildings of different heights. A naive subdivision method that concentrates on the 2D layout of the city might end up with most view cells seeing the whole city, because the upper parts of all view cells extend over the roof tops. Clearly we would like to separate these regions from those which see only the nearby streets. This shows that even for relatively simple types of scenes, important visibility changes can occur due to the height structure of the model.

The only published methods dealing with this problem are either based on very simple regular top-down subdivision schemes, or treat only special types of scenes (for more details refer to Section 2.4.1.1). In many practical applications (e.g., computer games), designers do not rely on automatic methods for view cell construction but tweak them by hand to meet certain constraints concerning PVS size or memory footprint. The finest possible subdivision is given by the aspect graph, which partitions the view space into cells from which the qualitative aspect of the scene does not change [PD90]. However, the full aspect graph requires as much as $O(n^9)$ nodes for perspective views (n is number of polygonal edges) and is therefore prohibitively expensive to compute and to store.

What is even more surprising is that the problem of finding a good set of objects for preprocessed visibility has practically not been addressed. Previous methods would either (a) use scene triangles, which is impractical with

3.2. Global visibility sampling

modern GPUs and prohibitively expensive both in memory cost and visibility computation time, (b) assume that the objects are given, which is not always the case, e.g. with large unprocessed datasets originating from a laser scan, or (c) use traditional object-space partitioning techniques like a bounding volume hierarchy with the surface area heuristics.

Using traditional object-space partitioning techniques is a viable option, but does not take into account that view space and object space are visibility dependent and also interdependent. The resulting set of objects directly influences the quality of the preprocessed visibility information. If the partitioning is too fine, the memory costs for storing preprocessed visibility will be very high. Additionally the setup costs for rendering the corresponding fine-grained objects on the GPU will become a burden. On the other hand if the partitioning is too coarse, visibility information will be inaccurate, leading to more geometry being rendered than necessary, and therefore slower frame rates.

In our algorithms, we sample actual visibility information about the scene to drive our heuristics. This sampling process is one of the key steps of our methods, and we discuss it in detail in the following section.

3.2 Global visibility sampling

The first step in our approaches is to sample the whole view space sufficiently to obtain a coarse, but reliable estimate of the visibility in a scene. A view space sample is a 5D entity corresponding to a ray in primal space. For simplicity, let's assume that the view space is defined by a 3D spatial box of possible ray origins (*view space box*) and contains all possible ray directions. The view space is then sampled using the following strategy:

1. Determine an origin point P and a direction d of a random sample.

2. Cast a 'forward' ray from p in direction d and a 'backward' ray from p in the opposite direction $-d$.

3. Construct a line segment formed by the calculated termination points

Chapter 3. Algorithms for Scene Preprocessing

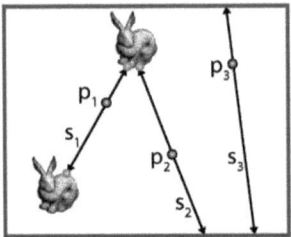 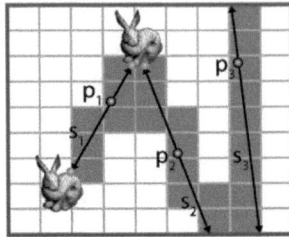

Figure 3.1: (left) Illustration of the determination of visibility segments. (right) The object information carried by the segments is then associated with the view cells they intersect (shown in green).

of the forward and backward rays. If at least one of the two rays hits an object, we call the resulting line segment a valid *visibility segment* and store it for later use.

The determination of visibility segments is illustrated in Figure 3.1. Three visibility samples are generated from points p_1, p_2 and p_3, resulting in two valid visibility segments. s_1 carries information about the visibility of two objects, s_2 about one object. s_3 is not a valid visibility segment since it does not hit any object. The PVS for a view cell is computed as a union of objects associated with the visibility segments intersecting the view cell (Figure 3.1 right).

Each sample is a line segment which associates all points on the line segment with the visibility of the object(s) on its endpoints. Samples are bound by the intersection points determined by the ray casting algorithm on each side. If the ray caster reports no intersection, we clip the ray to the view space bounding box.

There is an interesting subtlety involved in polygon orientations. For a general scene, the above procedure will create visibility segments in the interiors of objects if those regions are not explicitly exempted from view space. If, however, the input model is guaranteed to be watertight and the polygons have a consistent orientation, the algorithm can detect *empty view space* at no additional cost: if a ray hits the back side of a polygon, the ray

3.2. Global visibility sampling

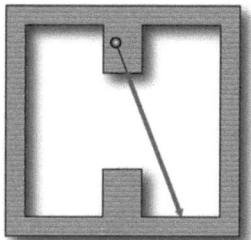

Figure 3.2: Example of empty view space detection. The origin of the ray lies inside the wall of the building and so the ray first hits a back-facing polygon. We shift the ray origin to the intersection point and re-cast it. The resulting visibility segment is shown as a thick line.

starting point is simply shifted to the intersection point and the ray is re-cast (see Figure 3.2). In this way, no visibility segments will be generated in empty space. We have found that empty view space detection can improve the final solution, because visibility regions are more clearly separated.

3.2.1 Sample distributions

For a reliable visibility estimate, the sampling should be roughly uniformly distributed in view space, in the sense that the density of samples is distributed more or less equally in the scene. There are several possible strategies for generating randomly distributed samples. The most intuitive strategy is the *point-direction* distribution [BMW*09], where we choose a random point and direction that define the sample.

Alternatively we can choose a start point on an object surface and cast the ray towards the view cells which see the object. The ray origins are distributed uniformly over the object surface, and the ray directions use a cosine weighted distribution over the object surfaces.

Interestingly, the best sampling strategy in our experiments was the so called *two-point* distribution [BMW*09], where we randomly select two points in the view space that can be used to determine the sampling origin and direction. It seems that this strategy reflects the distribution of potential locations

Chapter 3. Algorithms for Scene Preprocessing

of visible objects better than directionally uniform sampling. For example, if directionally uniform sampling is used in city-like scenes, many samples either hit the ground or the sky and thus provide no useful information about visible objects.

The samples are generated using a 5D Halton sequence in order to provide samples with low discrepancy. For more information on different static sampling strategies, please refer to the work of Bittner et al. [BMW*09]. Note that due to occlusion, none of these strategies generates fully uniform samples. To achieve full uniformity we would have to use global lines [SPNP96], which are much more expensive to generate. Therefore we suggest to use a mixture of some of these sampling strategies in order to avoid biasing. Next we propose two specific algorithms that use the sampling information for intelligent scene preprocessing.

3.3 Problem definition

The input to our algorithms is a subset $VS \subseteq \mathbf{R}^3$ called view space, and a set $OS \subseteq \mathbf{N}$ of object identifiers representing the geometric primitives in the scene. The algorithm operates on *partitions* (or subdivisions) of VS and OS, called $\mathcal{V}$ and $\mathcal{O}$ respectively. Initially, $\mathcal{V} = \{VS\}$. $\mathcal{O}$ is assumed to be given for the first algorithm, while we start with $\mathcal{O} = \{OS\}$ for the second algorithm. Each step in the first algorithm *splits* one node in V, while each step in the second algorithm splits exactly one node in *either* $\mathcal{V}$ or $\mathcal{O}$. An object space split of node $O = O_1 + O_2$, for example, transforms the partition $\mathcal{O}$ into $\mathcal{O}' = (\mathcal{O} \setminus \{O\}) \cup \{O_1, O_2\}$. The goal of both algorithms is to globally reduce a cost function corresponding to the expected rendering time to a minimum as induced by V and O (i.e., for visibility solutions based on the calculated subdivisions), while respecting certain constraints like the maximum memory footprint.

3.3. Problem definition

3.3.1 Render cost model

The render cost c_r of a given view space and object space partition $\mathcal{V}$ and $\mathcal{O}$ is given by the expected value of the rendering time over all view cells:

$$c_r(\mathcal{V}, \mathcal{O}) = \sum_{V \in \mathcal{V}} p(V) r(PVS_V), \; PVS_V \subseteq \mathcal{O} \quad (3.1)$$

where PVS_V is an approximate PVS of view cell V consisting of objects from $\mathcal{O}$, $r(PVS_V)$ is a rendering time estimator [WW03] for this PVS, and $p(V)$ is the probability of the viewpoint being located in view cell V. Assuming that viewpoints will be distributed uniformly in the whole view space, $p(V)$ can be chosen as the ratio of the volume Vol_V of the given view cell and the total volume Vol_{tot} of the view space:

$$p(V) = \frac{Vol_V}{Vol_{tot}}.$$

Alternatively, the user can specify any probability density d for viewpoint locations, so that areas where the user is more likely to move receive more attention in the view cell construction. $p(V)$ is then given by:

$$p(V) = \frac{\int_V d(V)}{\int_{VS} d(V)}.$$

The rendering time for a view cell is estimated from the rendering times for the objects in the PVS as seen from view cell V:

$$r(PVS_V) = \sum_{O \in PVS_V} \bar{r}(O, V).$$

The rendering time estimation function $\bar{r}(O, V)$ is difficult to establish exactly, since it depends not only on the particular set of objects, their attributes and distance to the view cell V, but also on the actual implementation and hardware. On the other hand, the view cell subdivision should not be tied too much to a specific hardware, neither do we have an accurate PVS (it is only estimated from a coarse visibility sampling) to determine the absolute value of the rendering time. Therefore we propose to loosely calibrate an analytic rendering time estimation function [WW03] to a small

Chapter 3. Algorithms for Scene Preprocessing

number of target machines. Since current graphics hardware is CPU limited for small batches, the following function provides good results:

$$\bar{r}(O, V) = \max(a, bt_O, cp_O),$$

where a, b and c are positive constants, and t_O and p_O are the number of triangles and the number of projected pixels of object o (estimated from some points in the cell) respectively.

3.4 Adaptive visibility-driven view cell construction

Our first algorithm assumes that scene objects are already given and allows for an automatic partitioning of view space into a multi-level view cell hierarchy. Our subdivision process has a sufficient degree of freedom to align the split planes with the scene geometry, but unlike some previous methods the partition is not restricted to planes given by the scene geometry. We show that the resulting view cell hierarchy works for different types of scenes and gives lower average rendering time than previously used methods.

3.4.1 What is a good view cell partition?

First we have to establish what criteria determine a "good" view cell partition, and explain why we chose to use this particular render cost model described in Section 3.3.1 for our subdivision process. Since the ultimate goal of visibility preprocessing is to accelerate rendering, the runtime *render costs* will play an important role. The intuitive answer is that the partition should *minimize* the render costs at runtime for each possible viewpoint. A view cell subdivision corresponding to this criterion actually exists and is given by the aspect graph. This structure is fully determined by the visibility structure of the scene, namely by the so-called visual events (boundaries at which changes in visibility occur). However, this subdivision would be prohibitively expensive to compute and to store.

3.4. Adaptive visibility-driven view cell construction

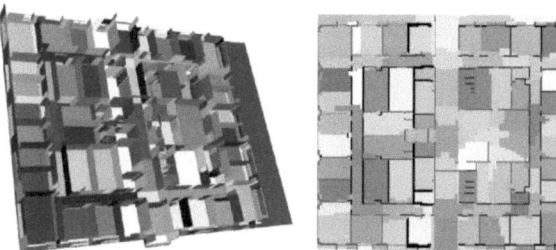

Figure 3.3: Right: A 2D cut through a set of view cells constructed with our method for the Soda Hall building (through the floor shown on the left). Note how the shape of view cells adapts to loci of visibility events.

This leads to *PVS storage space* and *precomputation time* as further important criteria. Both of these are determined by the total number of view cells in the subdivision, the actual visibility, the visibility algorithm, and the PVS storage method used: output-sensitive visibility algorithms can make computation time sublinear in the number of view cells, and PVS compression schemes can significantly reduce the required storage space.

An alternative to minimizing runtime render costs is to specify a rendering budget, i.e., a *maximum render cost* for a view cell. However, a model can contain an arbitrary number of viewpoints for which this rendering budget cannot be met. This can easily lead to excessive subdivision in areas with unrestricted visibility, and therefore again to high storage costs and precomputation time. Furthermore, such a view cell partition will be strongly tied to a particular runtime system, which is undesirable for a preprocessing algorithm.

We therefore propose the *average (= expected) render cost* of the whole view space as the criterion to drive the view cell construction (as defined in Equation 3.1), because it can be well combined with a constraint on the number of view cells in order to limit PVS storage costs and precomputation time.

We have to choose the shape of the candidate view cells that will be subjected to the above criteria. One option is a regular subdivision (e.g., a

Chapter 3. Algorithms for Scene Preprocessing

kD-tree of the scene). However, the boundaries of such view cells will not coincide with actual changes in visibility, i.e., visual events. On the other hand, finding these visual events (e.g., using the aspect graph) is expensive. We therefore propose a two-tier approach: an initial subdivision will follow (but not be restricted by) the geometry in the scene. Cells of this initial subdivision will subsequently be merged according to the visibility information in the scene. This causes the final view cells to approximate the important visual events in the scene.

Our adaptive view cell construction technique takes the actual visibility structure of the scene into account, and relies on four novel contributions: (1) the visibility of the scene is approximated by an inexpensive stochastic sampling step, (2) the view cell construction is driven by the average rendering time of the resulting partition, which is ultimately the most important factor in visibility processing, (3) an optimized set of view cells is found by combining top-down subdivision and bottom-up merging steps, and (4) our method allows easy control over the subdivision by using intuitive global termination criteria such as a threshold on rendering time reduction or a maximum memory budget. Another novelty is that we do not construct a fixed set of view cells, but provide a hierarchy of view cells, which makes it easy to extract an optimized set of view cells for a given set of constraints. As a result, our view cell subdivision provides fast rendering times with a minimal set of view cells, thus saving both preprocessing time and PVS storage space. See Figure 3.3 for an example of a view cell partition created with our technique.

3.4.2 Overview

3.4.2.1 Algorithm outline

Our view cell construction method consists of three main steps:

1. Visibility sampling

2. View space subdivision

3.4. Adaptive visibility-driven view cell construction

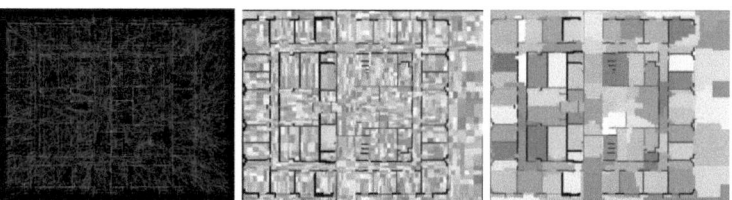

Figure 3.4: (left) Visibility segments determined by the visibility sampling step; 5000 of 1M line segments are depicted for sake of clarity. (center) Initial view space subdivision consisting of 5000 view cells. (right) 200 view cells retrieved from the merge history tree.

3. View space merging

The first step estimates visibility in the scene, which allows basing the view cell construction on scene visibility without incurring the overhead of having to calculate an accurate visibility solution. The resulting maximal free line segments (i.e., the visibility segments introduced in Section 3.2)) provide information about scene visibility for the subsequent steps of the view cells construction.

The second step performs an adaptive hierarchical subdivision of view space. The subdivision is driven by heuristics which aim to minimize the estimated render cost of the resulting subdivision. The result is a set of elementary view cells which satisfy certain global termination criteria (maximum memory budget or minimal render cost reduction).

The third step merges the elementary view cells to larger ones while minimizing the increase of the estimated render cost for each merging step. The merging progress is recorded in a *merge history tree*. The initial subdivision and the merge history define a *view cell hierarchy*, which allows retrieving an optimal set of view cells for a specified granularity of the view space subdivision. Additionally, this hierarchy can be used to compress the PVSs in a simple and efficient way. The merging step will implicitly approximate important visibility events in the scene. The three steps of our algorithm are illustrated in Figure 3.4.

Chapter 3. Algorithms for Scene Preprocessing

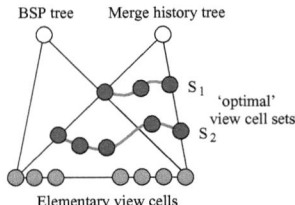

Figure 3.5: The view cell hierarchy is represented using a BSP tree and the merge history tree. The BSP tree provides a geometrical description for elementary view cells. The merge history tree provides a logical grouping of the view cells, which allows extracting a set of view cells with a specified granularity of the subdivision. The example shows two sets $\mathcal{S}_1$ and $\mathcal{S}_2$, where the desired number of view cells for $\mathcal{S}_2$ is larger than for $\mathcal{S}_1$.

3.4.2.2 Representation of view cells

We maintain the view space partition as a binary space partition tree which is constructed top-down. The leaves of this tree are convex polyhedra which form a set of elementary view cells. The final view cell partition is constructed from these elementary view cells using a bottom-up merging procedure which is recorded in a merge history tree. Note that merging is not tied to the original subdivision and therefore usually results in a different, more optimal tree. Both steps of the view cell hierarchy construction will be detailed in the next section. The representation of view cells using the two hierarchies is shown in Figure 3.5.

Note that we partition the view space only in the spatial domain, since the observer can quickly move through the whole directional space within a few frames by changing the viewing direction. Fortunately, culling in directional space is efficiently handled by view-frustum culling.

3.4.3 Adaptive view cell construction

In this section we describe the view space construction using the sampled visibility information. First we describe the subdivision process of the view

3.4. Adaptive visibility-driven view cell construction

space, then the further optimization of the view cells in a subsequent merging process.

3.4.3.1 View space subdivision

The view space subdivision uses a top-down approach to create a set of elementary view cells. In particular we use *binary space partitioning* (BSP) maintained by a BSP tree. Starting with a single view cell corresponding to the whole view space, we recursively subdivide the current view cell using either axis-aligned planes or planes aligned with scene geometry. Each cell of the subdivision also references all visibility segments that intersect it.

The BSP construction uses greedy optimization for the next-best split. Note that in contrast to most previous work on BSP or kD-tree construction, we employ a priority queue for selecting the splitting plane candidates. An entry in the priority queue consists of a reference to a leaf node, the best splitting plane candidate inside this leaf, and a cost reduction which would be achieved when splitting the leaf by the plane. For each step of the subdivision, we select the node for which its best splitting plane provides the highest render cost reduction. The subdivision is thus refined progressively and regions with the highest potential render cost decrease are subdivided first.

The best splitting plane for a node is established as follows: we generate axis-aligned splitting plane candidates positioned at the endpoints of rays intersecting the node. Additionally, we generate planes aligned with the geometry contained in that node (if any). For each candidate, we calculate the reduction of the expected rendering cost $c_r(\mathcal{S})$ that would result from subdividing the node by that plane. This is done by partitioning the current set of visibility segments according to the plane (note that a segment can be assigned to both sets), computing the PVSs (i.e., the union of the objects hit by the visibility segments) for the front and back segment sets, and using those to evaluate the reduction of the cost. Finally, we choose the candidate plane that provides the most reduction in expected render cost and put a corresponding entry in the priority queue. The subdivision is terminated

Chapter 3. Algorithms for Scene Preprocessing

when one of the following termination criteria is met:

- A specified maximum number of elementary view cells have been generated. This ensures that the algorithm stays within reasonable memory bounds.

- The cost reduction for the best splitting plane is below a specified threshold. As the cost reduction can temporarily stagnate, we only terminate when the reduction was below the threshold in several successive subdivision steps.

Due to the priority-driven subdivision, the view space will be evenly subdivided regardless of the termination point. This is not the case for depth-first approaches, where for example a termination on low memory would leave whole view space regions unsubdivided. Additionally, the local termination criteria used in the depth-first approach are hard to tune.

We experienced that in some rare cases the described greedy optimization can lead into a local minimum. Consider the situation that the render cost of a node cannot be reduced by the current split, but only by subsequent splits of the child nodes. However, the node is never chosen for subdivision because it provides no render cost decrease. We have addressed this problem by computing a weighted sum of the render cost reduction and the absolute render cost of the node in the evaluation of its priority. A very small weight of the absolute render cost (1%) has been sufficient to ensure that the split is taken at some point during subdivision.

Note that the time required for the subdivision is dominated by the cost evaluation for the candidate planes. To accelerate this process, we limit the number of axis-aligned as well as geometry-aligned candidates. If the number of visibility segments or geometry planes is above these limits, we select their random subsets. This speeds up the selection especially for nodes near the root of the subdivision tree.

3.4. Adaptive visibility-driven view cell construction

3.4.3.2 View space merging

View space merging is a bottom-up process which aims to reduce the number of view cells while minimizing the cost of the merged view cell set. We use a greedy algorithm that always merges the pair of view cells resulting in the minimal cost increase. This is done by maintaining a priority queue of view cell merge candidates. Each pair of neighboring view cells forms a merge candidate. The cost increase due to the merge candidate consisting of view cells x and y is given as:

$$\Delta_{c_r}(x,y) = c_r(\{x \oplus y\}) - c_r(\{x,y\}), \qquad (3.2)$$

where $x \oplus y$ is the view cell resulting from merging the set of view cells $\{x,y\}$. The priority of the merge candidate is then given by $-\Delta_{c_r}(x,y)$.

In the beginning, the queue is initialized with all pairs of neighboring view cells. At every step, we select the merge candidate with the highest priority (smallest relative cost increase) and merge the associated view cells. The PVS and the estimated render cost of the new view cell is calculated. After the merge, the priority queue is updated by removing entries corresponding to the merged view cells and inserting new entries corresponding to the created view cell and its neighbors. Note that the set of neighbors for a view cell is determined using the BSP tree.

The merging process provides a sequence of view cell sets: at every merge step we obtain a new set of view cells with exactly one view cell less than in the previous set. We record the whole merging process in a merge history tree. The leaves of this tree correspond to elementary view cells. Every internal node corresponds to a merged view cell. With each internal node we associate the current cost of the subdivision resulting from the corresponding merge.

Once the merge history tree is built, there are several ways how to create a view cell partition from the tree. The easiest way is to specify a target number n of view cells and extract these from the tree (for more detail see Section 3.4.4). These view cells can then be used as input for a visibility preprocessing algorithm.

Chapter 3. Algorithms for Scene Preprocessing

3.4.4 Using the view cell hierarchy

This section discusses different possibilities for using the constructed view cell hierarchy.

3.4.4.1 Extracting view cells

The view cell hierarchy allows extracting the set of view cells most suitable for the target application. Below we discuss three possibilities of view cell extraction.

Getting a specified number of view cells. Often, it is most convenient to specify a desired number of view cells to use for visibility calculation. This limits both the preprocessing time and the storage required for PVS data, as well as restricting the frequency with which new PVS data has to be fetched due to crossing into a new view cell at runtime. To obtain a given number of view cells, we perform a priority traversal of the merge history tree. The priority of a node is given by the cost associated with the node. When reaching a leaf node, we add it to the list of resulting view cells. When the sum of traversed leaves and the nodes in the priority queue becomes equal to the desired number of view cells, we terminate the traversal and add the contents of the priority queue to the resulting view cells. The collected view cells form a cut of the merge history tree at optimal depths with respect to the specified granularity.

Fulfilling a given memory budget. The procedure described above can be extended to allow specifying an approximate memory budget for the complete PVS representation (it is only approximate because it relies on the approximate PVS from the sampling step). At every step of the tree traversal, we can easily calculate the memory requirements for the current set of view cells and their approximate PVSs. We can terminate the traversal when the budget is reached and collect the resulting view cells as described above. Note that this step can also be applied after computing the final visibility classification. In this case the memory budget would be the real budget for storing the PVS representation.

Extracting important view cells. An alternative to the methods described

3.4. Adaptive visibility-driven view cell construction

above is view cell extraction based on their estimated render cost. In particular we can use the maximal tolerance of the increase of the estimated render cost over the minimal cost, i.e., the cost provided by the densest view space partition (elementary view cells). The view cells are extracted again by a priority traversal of the merge history tree. At each step we evaluate the ratio of the current cost (stored with the processed node) and the minimal cost. If the ratio falls below a threshold, we terminate the traversal and collect the resulting view cells as described above.

Interactive specification. In practice, the user can combine these methods in an interactive setup. The selection process can easily be accomplished with a real-time visualization of the view cells and a depiction of the associated cost and memory budgets, as well as the just described cost ratio. Typically, the user would start by setting an initial cost ratio and refining the result interactively. This allows the user interactive control over the process, which is a feature often desired by practitioners.

3.4.4.2 PVS compression

Due to spatial coherence, the siblings in the hierarchy will have mostly coherent PVSs. In order to further reduce the memory footprint of the view cells, we can propagate the PVS information as high in the hierarchy as possible [GSF99] once we have calculated the actual PVSs using a visibility preprocessing algorithm. The intersection of the PVSs of the children is propagated to the parent and deleted from the children, which reduces the number of references stored at the leaves.

3.4.5 Results

We have evaluated our method on three test scenes. The first scene (Soda) represents the Soda Hall building, the second scene (Atlanta) represents 30km^2 of Atlanta, and the third scene (Vienna) represents the city of Vienna (see Figure 3.6). The Soda scene consists of 9129 objects formed directly by the scene polygons, the Atlanta scene of 3495 objects (100k polygons), and the used version of the Vienna scene of 12668 objects (1M polygons).

Chapter 3. Algorithms for Scene Preprocessing

Figure 3.6: We tested our view cell construction algorithm in typical city scenes (left, Vienna) and building interiors. The right image shows a snap shot of an interactive render cost visualization from a view point outside of the Soda Hall building, on a scale from green (view cells with low render cost) to red (high render cost). The geometry is shown as a wireframe.

3.4.5.1 Evaluation Framework

In our experiments we have observed that evaluating the view space partition by visual inspection is difficult. Often such an inspection can even be misleading: nicely looking view cells like those corresponding to corridors in a building, are bad in terms of the render cost. As a basic tool for evaluating the quality of the partition we use the dependence of the expected render cost on the number of view cells. For selected tests, we also use histograms which show the distribution of render cost among view cells for a specified granularity.

In order to compare different view cell construction strategies, we cast additional *evaluation* samples (rays) after the view cells have been constructed. The only purpose of the evaluation samples is to obtain comparable render cost estimations. These samples determine PVSs for all view cells of the view cell hierarchy, which are then used for evaluating Equation 3.1. Note that although the number of evaluation samples we used is larger than the number of initial samples, the computed PVSs are still only approximations to the exact ones. For methods which don't use view space merging, the view cell hierarchy is just defined by the initial subdivision step.

3.4. Adaptive visibility-driven view cell construction

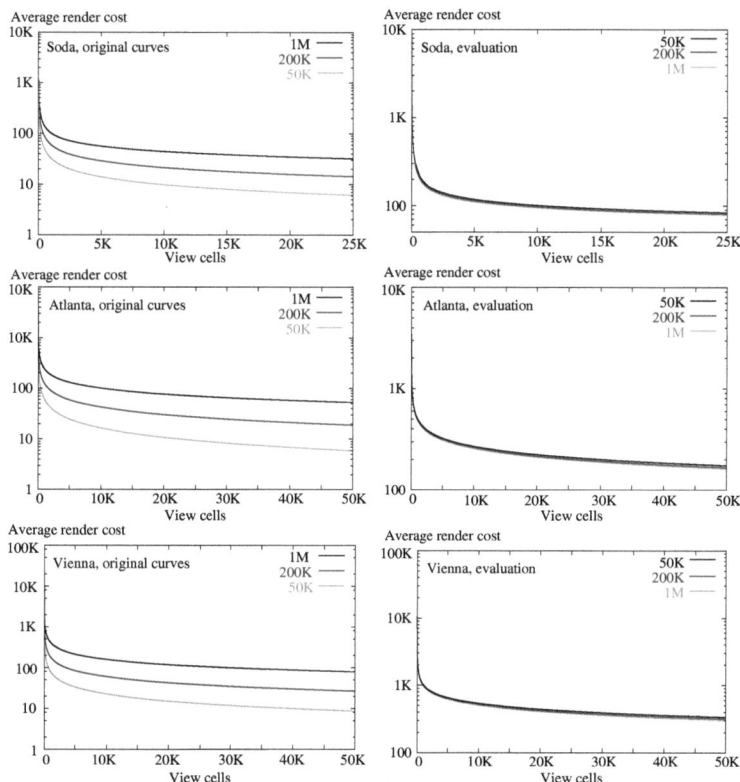

Figure 3.7: Evaluation of visibility sampling. The left columns of plots shows the actual render cost estimates for the Soda, Atlanta and Vienna scenes for subdivisions created from 50k, 200k, and 1M visibility samples. The right columns shows a verification of the resulting subdivisions by using 8M evaluation samples. From top to bottom: Soda, Atlanta, and Vienna scene.

Chapter 3. Algorithms for Scene Preprocessing

3.4.5.2 Visibility sampling

The first test aims to verify our assumption that a relatively coarse visibility sampling is sufficient to establish a stable render cost estimate for driving the view space partition. In order to evaluate this, we have constructed view space subdivisions using different numbers of visibility samples (50k, 200k, 1M). The results are summarized in Figure 3.7. As expected, lower numbers of visibility samples generate lower render cost estimates due to visibility undersampling. However, by casting the same number of evaluation samples, we can observe that the resulting subdivisions provide comparable render costs. For example there is only a minor improvement by moving from 200k to 1M samples.

3.4.5.3 Comparison with other methods

In Figure 3.8, we show a comparison with other proposed view cell construction methods. We compared 7 different view cell construction methods: our method with view space merging (AV-M), our method without view space merging (AV-S), breadth-first kD-tree subdivision using spatial median split and along a cycling axis (KD-CASM), breadth-first kD-tree subdivision using spatial median split and along the longest axis (KD-LASM), depth-first kD-tree subdivision along the longest axis with additional visibility-based termination (i.e., the number of PVS entries is smaller than a user-defined threshold) (KD-VT) and BSP subdivision aligned with the scene geometry (BSP). For our method we cast 1.5M rays to generate visibility samples. Note that BSP corresponds to the method for cell and portal construction described by Teller [Tel92b], where a node is split by aligning the split plane with the largest polygon intersecting the node (and terminating the subdivision if there is no such polygon left), also known as auto-partition BSP algorithm. KD-VT corresponds to subdivisions performed by Saona-Vázquez et al. [SVNB99] and Nirenstein et al. [NB04a] for visibility preprocessing in general scenes. We describe these algorithms in more detail in Section 2.4.1.

The results for three different test scenes are summarized in Figure 3.8. A number of observations can be made from the measured results:

3.4. Adaptive visibility-driven view cell construction

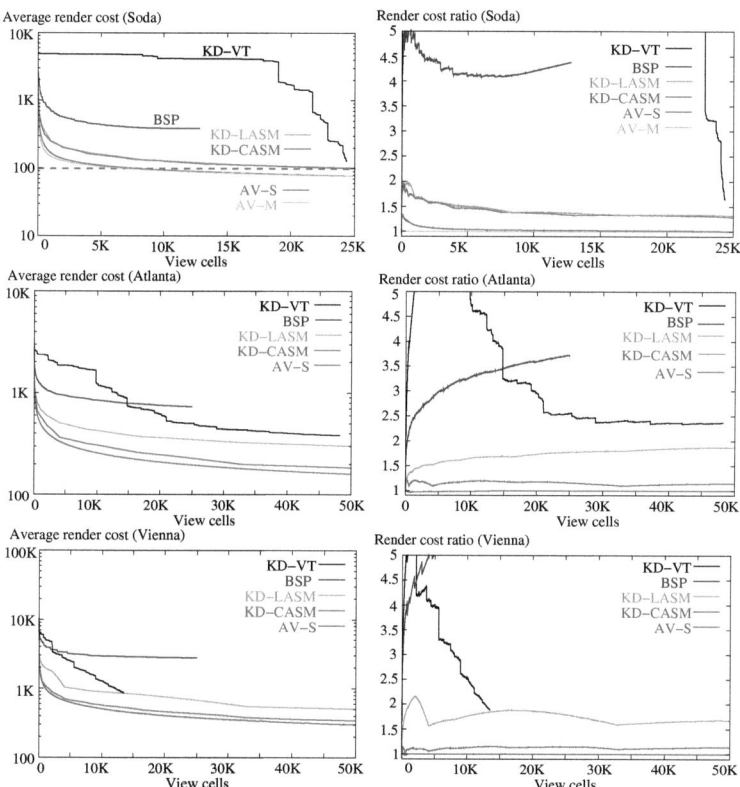

Figure 3.8: Comparison of the different view cell construction methods for three different scenes (from top to bottom: Soda, Atlanta, Vienna). The left column shows the expected render cost depending on the number of view cells. The right column shows the render cost ratio with respect to our AV-M method.

Chapter 3. Algorithms for Scene Preprocessing

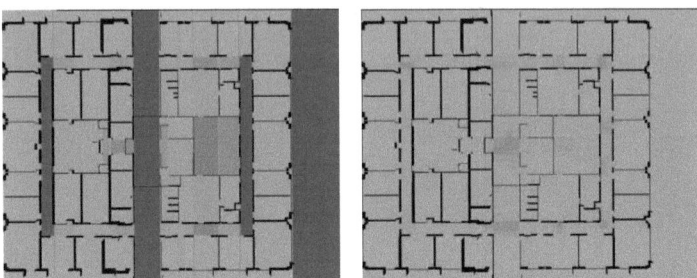

Figure 3.9: (left) BSP based view cells have the problem that large regions with high PVS (shown in dark/magenta) are not subdivided any further, while (right) our method nicely subdivides these regions.

- Our method performs better than the comparison methods in all tests. The gain over the best reference method (KD-CASM) in terms of the render cost is about 20-30%.

- The gain of view space merging (AV-M) applied on our subdivision (AV-S) is very limited. The only benefit appears in the Soda scene for a lower number of view cells. Therefore we show the AV-M curve only for this scene.

- KD-CASM performs significantly better than KD-LASM in outdoor city scenes. In these scenes, horizontal subdivision of view cells is very important, as it separates regions with complex visibility which see above the roofs of the buildings from those which see only the nearby streets. When using KD-LASM, the horizontal splits occur only for a very high density of the subdivision.

- The plots show that BSP performs worst of the tested methods, as it cannot provide a sufficient reduction of the render cost. This follows from the inability of auto-partition BSP to subdivide regions with high render cost, which however contain no geometry that can be used to align the split plane. This observation is not surprising for the Atlanta scene and the Vienna scene, as the method is not designed for outdoor

3.4. Adaptive visibility-driven view cell construction

scenes. However, even in inside the Soda building the BSP method leaves large view cells corresponding to the corridors with complex visibility, which intuitively look like good view cells but have very high render cost. On the other hand as shown in Figure 3.9, our method successfully subdivides these high PVS regions. We subdivided down to 2734 leaves for both methods.

- The depth-first subdivision (KD-VT) arrives at a termination point with a cost of 50-80% higher than that of our method for the same number of view cells. However, as seen from the plot, it does not provide a scalable solution with respect to the number of view cells. This problem can be addressed by a breadth-first modification of the method. Similarly to KD-LASM, KD-VT also splits at the spatial median of the longest axis. With breadth-first subdivision, the resulting render cost curves for both methods are practically the same. Note that we used a relatively low PVS termination criterion, otherwise the subdivision is often terminated much too early, with many objects missed by the coarse sampling, resulting in view cells with high render cost in the fully computed visibility solution.

- Another criterion for evaluating the methods is the number of view cells needed to achieve the same render cost. We can see that the reference methods need significantly larger numbers of view cells in order to reach the same render cost as the AV-S or AV-M methods. Also note that for some methods, a particular render cost cannot be reached within a given view cell budget. For example, in the upper right plot of Figure 3.8 a render cost of 100 (indicated by the brown line) is reached by our methods after less than 8000 view cells, while about 25000 view cells are required for the next best methods, and the other methods never seem to reach this point.

We have also compared the breadth-first version of the KD-VT and AV-M methods, using a histogram showing the distribution of render cost over the view space volume (see Figure 3.10). For the AV-M method, most of

Chapter 3. Algorithms for Scene Preprocessing

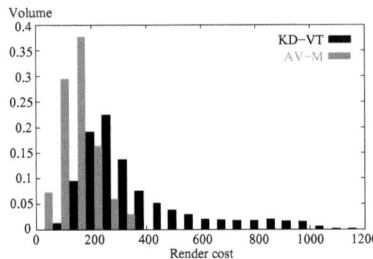

Figure 3.10: Render cost / volume histogram for the AV-M and KD-VT (breadth-first) methods computed for the Vienna scene with 15000 view cells.

the volume is covered by lower render cost. In contrast, the KD-VT method still contains numerous regions with high render cost: there are regions with up to 3 times higher render cost compared to the maximum render cost for the AV-M method. This observation indicates that even if AV-M does not provide an impressive reduction of the average render cost, it results in a significantly better render cost distribution over the view space volume.

3.4.5.4 Using view space merging on existing solutions

View space merging can be applied as a standalone technique for obtaining a scalable view cell representation from an existing set of view cells. An example of this process is shown in Figure 3.11 (left). We can see how the initial depth-first subdivision has been smoothed by the application of view space merging. Additionally the render cost curve resulting from the merging process gives us information about the required granularity of the subdivision. If many initial merging steps result only in a minor increase of the render cost, then we can safely reduce the number of view cells for the final visibility representation.

3.4.5.5 Influence of geometry-aligned splits

We have evaluated the influence of geometry-aligned splits on the expected render cost in non-axis aligned environments. In particular, we measured

3.4. Adaptive visibility-driven view cell construction

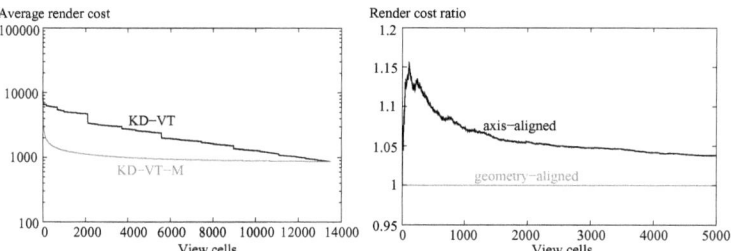

Figure 3.11: (left) View space merging applied on the subdivision using the KD-VT method. (right) Influence of geometry-aligned splits in a soda building rotated by 30 degrees. The plots shows the render cost ratio of using only axis-aligned splits with respect to a method using also geometry-aligned splits (render cost ratio=1).

the render cost curves for our method when using only axis-aligned splitting planes and when using also geometry-aligned planes. We limited the number of tested geometry-aligned split planes to 150. The result is summarized in Figure 3.11 (right). We can see that for this test the geometry-aligned planes give a benefit from 4 to 15%. This suggests that, when also taking into account the increased computational complexity connected with geometry-aligned splits, the benefit they provide is only marginal.

3.4.5.6 Timings

We have measured the running times of our view cell construction for several scenarios. The timings measured on a 3.4 GHz Intel Pentium 4 with 2GB of RAM are summarized in Table 3.1. We see that for more complex scenes, the time overhead due to geometry-aligned candidates as well as the time required for the merging increases. Since the benefit of these two techniques is relatively small in practice it should be sufficient to use our priority-driven subdivision using the cost heuristics and axis-aligned splits.

Chapter 3. Algorithms for Scene Preprocessing

Scene	Subdivision AA + GA [s]	Subdivision AA [s]	Merge [s]
Soda	430.8	287	103.3
Atlanta	1488	338.1	1912
Vienna	1565	354.1	1569

Table 3.1: Timings for generating 50000 view cells using our view cell construction method. For all tests we cast 1.5M rays to generate visibility samples. The table contains timings for the subdivision when using axis-aligned as well as geometry-aligned planes (AA + GA) and when using only the axis-aligned planes (AA). We limited the number of geometry-aligned candidate split planes to 150. The last column shows timings for the view space merging step.

3.4.6 Discussion

3.4.6.1 Visibility sampling

The idea which drives our view cell construction algorithm and which allows analyzing the quality of different view space subdivisions is visibility sampling and the usage of the visibility segments. As we have shown in the results, it is not necessary to calculate an accurate visibility solution for each step of the subdivision process in order to determine the following steps. Instead, even a relatively coarse sampling of visibility already gives stable estimates of the render cost. Our algorithm is therefore not limited by a slow visibility solver. It can quickly perform a deep top-down subdivision, which would not be possible if each subdivision step were to depend on the outcome of a complete visibility processing step.

3.4.6.2 Handling empty space

One of the important differences of our method compared to techniques designed for cell and portal graph construction is the handling of "empty space", i.e., regions which contain no geometry. The results show that even in indoor environments it is very important to further refine the subdivision in order to adapt to visibility (rendering) complexity. A purely geometry-based subdivision might result in big view cells which look "natural", but their PVS is way too large, even though a significant reduction is possible (as shown in Figure 3.9).

3.4.6.3 Handling difficult regions

The existing visibility preprocessing methods which perform adaptive view space partitioning [SVNB99, NB04a] handle difficult regions (i.e., regions with large irreducible PVS) by terminating subdivision at a specified maximal depth. This can be costly for preprocessing as well as storage. In our method this problem is addressed already at the subdivision stage and gets further refined in the merging step. The subdivision uses the cost-based global termination criterion which prevents further subdivision when all regions already have irreducible render cost. However there might be regions where the local benefit of the subdivision is just above the specified threshold. These regions will be merged soon in the merging stage, and thus the corresponding fragmented view cells will reside at the bottom of a merge history tree.

3.5 Optimized subdivisions for preprocessed visibility

In the previous section we proposed a tool for optimized view space partitioning. In this section, we extend this method to handle both view space and object space partitioning together in order to control the render cost and memory cost of the visibility description generated by a visibility solver. The presented method progressively refines view space and object space subdivisions while minimizing the associated render and memory costs. While we used actual visibility information to drive the view space subdivision in the previous section, this time *both* subdivisions are driven by actual visibility information. We show that treating view space and object space together provides a powerful method for controlling the efficiency of the resulting visibility data structures.

Chapter 3. Algorithms for Scene Preprocessing

Figure 3.12: Example of combined view space and object space subdivisions. The scene consists of a sphere inside the room which can be seen only through a small hole. We show a cut through the 3D view space subdivision. It concentrates in the regions which see the sphere through the hole and thus have higher render cost (low cost=blue, high cost=magenta). The partitioning of the geometry focuses on the front of the sphere which is visible from more view points.

This section provides two main contributions: 1) This is the first algorithm to consider object space subdivision as a visibility problem and which provides a solution for visibility driven object splits. 2) We present the first *integrated* visibility-based solution for view space subdivision and object space subdivision.

As a result, the expected render cost in the scene can be reduced significantly compared to a naive view space and object space subdivision. We will show that our algorithm consistently improves the render cost at a given memory cost, while naive methods are very fragile with respect to the relative depths of object and view space subdivisions. Figure 3.12 shows a simple illustrative example: using a non visibility-aware object subdivision method, the spherical object in the room would inevitably have been needlessly subdivided uniformly, whereas our method concentrates the subdivision to the front, where actual visibility events take place.

To our knowledge this method is the first which constructs an object space subdivision that is optimized for storing preprocessed visibility. The

3.5. Optimized subdivisions for preprocessed visibility

known visibility preprocessing methods assume that the objects are either (1) identical to the triangles, (2) defined in the modeling phase, or (3) result from a subdivision with some local termination criteria. In the first case the memory consumption of the resulting PVSs for scenes with many triangles and view cells are prohibitive. The second case requires manual modeling; additionally it is not obvious how well the results of modeling will fit the visibility data. In the third case the success of the preprocessing strongly depends on setting the termination criteria of the subdivision: if the partitioning is too fine, the memory costs for storing preprocessed visibility will be very high. If the partitioning is too coarse, there might be significant reserves in the render cost reduction and the desired frame rate will not be reached.

3.5.1 Outline

The basic idea of the proposed algorithm is the same as for the view cell construction algorithm from Section 3.4 – we acquire coarse visibility information about the scene in a global sampling step. Then we use this visibility information to partition view space and object space simultaneously.

The main criterion to drive the subdivision are the expected render and memory costs which are estimated from the coarse visibility information. Basically, each split attempts to reduce the render cost while keeping the associated memory cost increase as small as possible. As a result we end up with view space and object space subdivisions which can then be fed into any from-region visibility preprocessing algorithm. The proposed method thus consists of two main parts: visibility sampling and interleaved subdivision. *Visibility sampling* acquires visibility information which is represented as a set of maximal free line segments, which we call visibility segments (refer to Section 3.2). These segments are then used to quickly determine the visibility between the cells of the constructed view space and object space partitions.

The *subdivision* starts with a single view cell representing the whole view space and a single object representing the whole scene geometry. Both the view space and geometry partitions are progressively refined by splitting

Chapter 3. Algorithms for Scene Preprocessing

either a view cell or an object into two parts. The main criterion driving the splits are the expected render and memory costs which are estimated using visibility samples. Each split attempts to reduce the render cost while keeping the associated memory cost increase as small as possible.

Candidates for splitting are chosen from all current view cells *and* geometry nodes. The candidates are stored in a priority queue, and at each step we pick the candidate which provides the best ratio of render cost reduction over memory increase. This candidate is then used to subdivide the associated view space or object space cell. The subdivision proceeds until the given termination criteria are reached. In particular the algorithm terminates if the local render cost reduction falls below a specified threshold, or a maximal memory budget for the whole visibility data is reached. As a result the algorithm delivers optimized view space and object space partitions which can then be fed into any from-region visibility preprocessing algorithm.

3.5.2 Framework for interleaved subdivisions

The interleaved view space and object space partitioning, which is the core of the proposed method, is driven by a cost model based on the estimate of the average rendering time and the memory costs needed for storing the visibility information. This section describes a theoretical framework for the rest of the chapter. In particular it addresses the representation of the subdivisions, and evaluation of the render cost and the memory cost.

3.5.2.1 Representing the subdivisions

In our implementation, we use an axis-aligned kD-tree to represent the view space subdivision, with the leaf nodes corresponding to the view cells. As shown in Section 3.4, a kD-tree is efficient and provides good render cost reduction. To represent the object space subdivision, we use a bounding volume hierarchy. The hierarchy is a binary tree where each node recursively subdivides the associated triangles into two disjoint subsets represented by its two children. The leaves of the hierarchy correspond to the constructed scene objects. Each leaf (object) contains references to scene triangles. For

3.5. Optimized subdivisions for preprocessed visibility

each node we also keep an axis-aligned bounding box. Note that the bounding boxes of the leaves can be disjoint or overlap, but the structure has the advantage that each triangle is referred to only once and thus the memory consumption of the data structure is $O(n)$, as the internal nodes of the hierarchy only add a constant factor.

3.5.2.2 Render cost

The main factor in determining whether a split is beneficial or not is the effect such a split has on the *expected render cost* as defined in Section 3.3. For example, a view cell split often causes the child view cells to see less objects than the original cell, so that the render cost is lower in both cells. Similarly, an object space split can cause the resulting sub-objects to be present in the PVS of fewer view cells, similarly reducing the overall render costs.

3.5.2.3 Memory cost

While fine-grained partitions can reduce the render cost, they also increase memory costs. Therefore, memory costs need to be controlled. The memory cost c_m of a given set of view cells $\mathcal{V}$ and objects $\mathcal{O}$ is given by:

$$c_m(\mathcal{V}, \mathcal{O}) = M_V + M_O + M_{PVS}, \qquad (3.3)$$

where M_V is the memory needed to store the view cells, M_O is the memory needed to store the objects, and M_{PVS} is the memory for storing the PVSs, given as follows:

$$M_{PVS} = \sum_{V \in \mathcal{V}} \sum_{o \in PVS_V} m_e \qquad (3.4)$$

based on the elementary cost m_e of storing one object identifier.

3.5.3 Optimization approach

We cast the partitioning problem as an optimization problem. Let $\{(\mathcal{V}_i, \mathcal{O}_i) : i \in \mathbf{N}\}$ be the set of all possible view space and object space subdivisions

Chapter 3. Algorithms for Scene Preprocessing

resulting from splitting (we assume that there is only a finite number of possible split positions for each cell, and therefore this set is also finite). Then we look for a partition $(\mathcal{V}, \mathcal{O})$ with $c_r(\mathcal{V}, \mathcal{O}) = \min_i(c_r(\mathcal{V}_i, \mathcal{O}_i))$ and $c_m(\mathcal{V}, \mathcal{O}) \leq maxmem$, i.e., we look for the partition with the least render cost given a maximum allowed memory cost $maxmem$.

Enumerating all possible partitions would be prohibitively costly, and we therefore follow an idea borrowed from the well-known Knapsack problem [MT90]: a common greedy solution to the Knapsack problem always adds the element with the highest "value per size" ratio to the Knapsack. If we interpret the render cost decrease dR of a split as its "value", and the memory cost increase dM of a split as its "size", we can follow the same strategy.

We place all potential split candidates in a *priority queue* and calculate the priority of each candidate by the described ratio, i.e.,

$$p = \frac{dR}{dM}. \qquad (3.5)$$

The optimization algorithm therefore proceeds by repeatedly removing the split with the highest priority from the queue and applying it to the current partition. For the newly generated cells, new potential split candidates are added to the priority queue. This process is repeated until the maximum memory cost is reached. How the potential split candidates are obtained is described in Section 3.5.5.1.

Note that the algorithm does not distinguish between object space and view space splits – they are treated equally. The *memory cost increase* consists of a constant overhead of the split (new view cell or new object) on the one hand and the number of new PVS entries following from the split on the other hand. For example, when splitting an object, the PVS size of all view cells that see both sub-objects will be increased by m_e. The evaluation of the *render cost reduction* is described in the next section.

3.5. Optimized subdivisions for preprocessed visibility

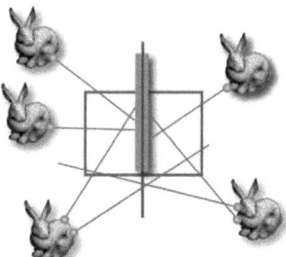

Figure 3.13: Illustration of a view space split. A view cell (light blue) is split by a plane which is aligned with the wall. The PVS breaks into two parts seen from the new view cells by the samples. Each part consists of objects seen from one of the view cells (blue and green shadows) and both view cells (cyan shadows).

3.5.3.1 Evaluating the render cost reduction

The crucial part of the algorithm is to evaluate the render cost reduction dR resulting from subdividing either view space or object space.

View space splits The render cost of a single view cell is defined as:

$$c_r(V) = p(V)r(PVS_V). \tag{3.6}$$

When subdividing a view cell V by a splitting plane, the render cost reduction is given by the difference of the render cost of the new view cells and the old one:

$$dR(V) = c_r(V_b) + c_r(V_f) - c_r(V) \tag{3.7}$$

where V_b and V_f are back and front fragments of the view cell V with respect to the splitting plane. The view space split is illustrated in Figure 3.13.

Object space splits To evaluate the render cost reduction when splitting an object, we first need to know from which view cells the object and its new fragments can be seen. We denote the set of view cells which can see an

Chapter 3. Algorithms for Scene Preprocessing

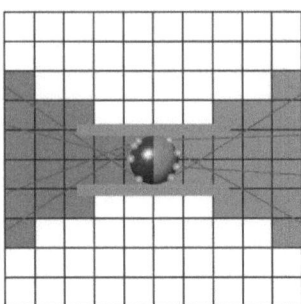

Figure 3.14: Illustration of an object space split. A spherical object inside a tube-like structure is subdivided into two parts shown in blue and green. In this example the view cells which see the object (by the samples) break into two disjoint sets.

object O as $\overline{PVS}_O$. The expected render cost of an object is then expressed as:

$$c_r(O) = \sum_{V \in \overline{PVS}_O} \bar{r}(O, V) p(V) \qquad (3.8)$$

where p(V) is the probability of the view point being located in view cell V and $\bar{r}(O,V)$ is the render cost of the object O seen from view cell V.

When subdividing an object O, the render cost reduction is given by:

$$dR(O) = c_r(O_b) + c_r(O_f) - c_r(O) \qquad (3.9)$$

where O_b and O_f are the back and front fragments of the object. The object space split is illustrated in Figure 3.14.

3.5.4 Visibility sampling

We gain information about global visibility in the scene by creating and using visibility samples used to estimate PVSs as described in Section 3.2. In the further steps of the algorithm, each sample is associated with an object resulting from the object space subdivision as well as a list of view

3.5. Optimized subdivisions for preprocessed visibility

cells resulting from the view space subdivision.

3.5.4.1 Dealing with visibility undersampling

Every leaf of the view space and object space hierarchies is associated with a set of visibility samples. For a view space node, this list consists of rays that intersect the corresponding view cell. For an object space node, this list consists of rays which are associated with triangles contained in the node. The PVS of a view space node (PVS_V) is enumerated as the union of all objects seen by the rays associated with the node. The PVS of an object space node ($\overline{PVS_O}$) is enumerated as the union of all view cells intersected by the associated rays.

In the beginning of the subdivision there are many visibility samples per node and the accuracy of the PVS estimation is relatively high. As the subdivision proceeds, there are less and less samples per node, and consequently the accuracy of the PVS estimation drops. As a result the estimated PVSs in the leaves can be significantly smaller than the real PVSs which would be obtained with an exact visibility solver.

To compensate for this visibility undersampling, we compute an *undersampling factor* for each subdivided node based on the number of rays intersecting the node and the size of the associated estimated PVS. This factor expresses the credibility of the PVSs computed for child nodes using the associated rays. We use this factor to correct the PVS size estimate as well as the render cost estimate for the nodes. The correction is done by blending the values computed using rays with the values determined for the parent node. If the number of rays is significantly larger than the PVS size (every object is sampled by many rays), we use the PVS and render cost without any correction. However, if the number of rays is comparable to the PVS size (every ray sees a different object) we use the PVS size and the render cost determined in the parent node. For cases between these two extremes we linearly interpolate between the values determined by the rays and those computed for the parent node.

Note that this correction is only an estimate, and therefore the total

Chapter 3. Algorithms for Scene Preprocessing

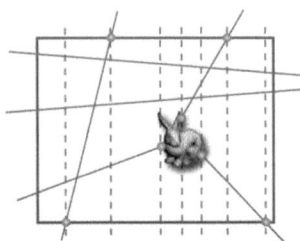

Figure 3.15: Establishing the split candidate for a view space node. The split planes are placed at the end-points of visibility samples inside the view cell and intersections of visibility samples with the view cell boundary. Then we pick the plane with highest priority as a split candidate for this node. The example shows only the split positions evaluated for one axis.

memory cost of the PVS calculated by the actual visibility solver can be larger than the bound *maxmem*.

3.5.5 Subdivision

This section describes in detail the selection of splitting planes, determination of their processing order, and the computation of the actual splits of view space or object space nodes.

3.5.5.1 Establishing split candidates

Whenever a new (object space or view space) cell is generated in the subdivision, we establish a new splitting plane candidate for this cell and add it to the priority queue. Within the cell, we aim to find the split plane with the highest priority according to Eq. 3.5. Both functions dR and dM have discontinuities at places of visibility changes (changes in PVS). The visibility changes can occur only at the end-points of the visibility samples clipped to the current node, i.e., either at an end-point of a visibility sample due to an object within the view cell, or at the intersection of a visibility sample with the view cell boundary. In order to achieve a high chance of separating the PVS, we compute these points and evaluate the split priorities for the

3.5. Optimized subdivisions for preprocessed visibility

corresponding split plane positions in all three axes. The splitting plane candidate for this node is then established at the position with highest priority. The selection of split plane candidate is illustrated in Figure 3.15.

To efficiently calculate the priorities for all positions, we use a sweeping plane algorithm as described in Section 3.4. We sort the positions and sweep the splitting plane along these positions. At every position of the plane, we compute the PVS incrementally by counting the references to objects seen by rays on both sides of plane. The priority for each position is then computed from the PVS using the formulas given in Section 3.5.3.1.

3.5.5.2 Processing split candidates

The split candidates established for every leaf of the current subdivision have to be processed in the order of descending priority. The basic algorithm described so far would just use a single priority queue of the candidates, pick the candidate with best priority, split the corresponding node and put split candidates for the newly created nodes into the priority queue. However, a view space split induces a change of the priorities of object space split candidates and vice versa. The affected candidates are those which could see the node that was split, i.e., those which are connected with that node with at least one ray. The priorities of the affected candidates have to be reevaluated and their position in the priority queue has to be updated. In the extreme case, a split of a single view space or object space node can affect all of the split candidates from the other domain (i.e., either view space or object space).

In order to cope with this situation, we exploit the following observation: when performing a split, the priority of other candidates in the queue remains valid if they are from the same domain as the split. This follows from the fact that the cost evaluation of disjoint nodes of the same domain is independent (at least for simple types of render cost evaluation functions). This means that recomputation is only necessary when switching domains from object to view space or vice versa. We use this observation to reduce the number of recomputations of split candidate priorities. The optimized algorithm

Chapter 3. Algorithms for Scene Preprocessing

maintains separate priority queues for split candidates of view space and object space domains and proceeds as follows:

Initially we take the split candidate with the highest priority by comparing the fronts of the view space and object space priority queues. We take at least n_{min} splits from the same domain *without reevaluation* of split candidate priorities. After $n_m in$ splits from one domain, we decide whether to switch based on the priorities of the two queue fronts. If the priority of the current split candidate is lower than the best split candidate from the other domain (condition 1), we recalculate the priorities of the candidates and decide whether to switch the domains. Otherwise we continue subdividing in the current domain until condition 1 is met or we reach n_{max} splits (condition 2). n_{max} is a safety criterion ensuring that reevaluation is made with sufficient frequency. As a result the number of steps without reevaluating the split candidate priorities is in the range (n_{min}, n_{max}).

Even when processing the splitting planes in batches, the update of all affected split candidates per batch is expensive. The deeper the subdivision, the more candidates have to be updated. To further reduce the number of recomputations of priorities, we only update a subset of split candidates. This subset is chosen randomly from the set of affected candidates.

We found that using a range of $(n_{min}, n_{max}) = (100, 900)$, and updating 2000 candidates per batch gives stable results. The final ratio of view space splits to object space splits is nearly independent from the range of n_{min} and n_{max}. The chosen settings are quite conservative, so taking less repair candidates will speed up the algorithm without significantly impacting the efficiency of the algorithm.

3.5.5.3 Splitting a node

The algorithm for the actual split of the node depends on the domain of the node. If a view space node is subdivided, we split the corresponding cell into two disjoint parts and create two new view cells (leaves of the kD-tree). Then we distribute the associated visibility samples to the new view cells using a line segment / box intersection tests. The visibility samples are

3.5. Optimized subdivisions for preprocessed visibility

used to compute the split candidates for the newly created nodes and their priorities. These split plane candidates are then inserted into the view space priority queue.

If an object space node is subdivided, we partition the triangles of the subdivided cell (object) into two disjoint sets based on the position of their center of mass with respect to the splitting plane. Then we distribute the visibility samples according to the position of the triangles stored with the rays in the child nodes. Similarly as for the view space splits, the visibility samples are used to compute the split plane candidates for the newly created nodes as well as their priorities. These split candidates are then inserted into the object space priority queue.

3.5.5.4 Initiating the subdivisions

Consider the situation that the whole view space is represented by a single view cell and all scene geometry is represented as a single object. If the view space and the object space are not disjoint, no reduction of the render cost can be achieved by either object or view space split, because either the view cell would intersect both new objects (which are then trivially contained in the PVS), or the single object would be contained in the PVSs of both new view cells because there is no other object which could act as an occluder.

In order to provide our heuristics some useful information about render cost reduction, we initiate the algorithm with coarse object space and view space subdivisions. The initial view space subdivision uses spatial median subdivision with cycling axis. The object space subdivision is performed using the SAH.

Alternatively the object space subdivision can apply a logical partition based on the size of the triangles or materials and shaders. A subdivision based on the size of the triangles separates large objects from small ones, which allows better separation of nodes of the constructed bounding volume hierarchy [KS06]. The initial partition according to materials and shaders has the advantage of keeping a limited number of shaders per leaf of the bounding volume hierarchy. In case of subdividing according to all materials

Chapter 3. Algorithms for Scene Preprocessing

Figure 3.16: Snapshot of the Arena scene from the outside (left) and inside the dome (right).

and shaders, all the triangles contained in a leaf of the bounding volume hierarchy can be displayed with a single render call.

Note that in general the initial logical partitions do not provide a good spatial separation of objects per se – the volumes corresponding to leaves of the hierarchy can largely overlap and even span the whole object space.

3.5.6 Results

We have evaluated the proposed method on two different scenes. The first scene (Vienna) represents $8km^2$ of the city of Vienna. The second scene (Arena) is a model of Sazka-Arena – a multipurpose stadium in Prague (courtesy of Digital Media Production a.s.) (see Figure 3.16). The Vienna scene consists of houses with windows and balconies, pavements, and roads. The Arena scene represents both the interior and the exterior of the stadium. The interior has high depth complexity (apart from the large open spaces, the building contains about 1000 rooms) and includes many instances of coarsely modeled objects such as chairs and tables. The Vienna scene contains 1M triangles, the Arena scene 1.5M triangles.

For both scenes we measured the dependence of the render cost estimate on the memory cost of the constructed subdivisions. As a reference for comparison, we used a method which initially subdivides object space using the surface area heuristics up to a specified number of objects, and then applies the visibility-driven view cell construction from Section 3.4 to subdivide view

3.5. Optimized subdivisions for preprocessed visibility

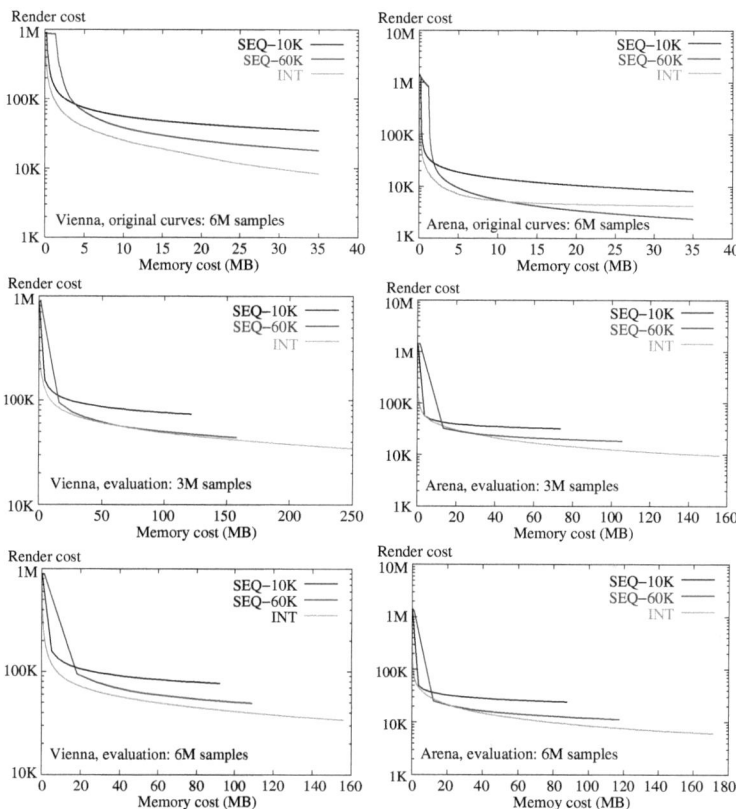

Figure 3.17: Render cost vs. memory cost curves for Vienna (left) and Arena (right). (top) Original curves, computed with 6M visibility samples. (center) Evaluation curves, computed with 3M visibility samples and measured using 160M evaluation samples. (bottom) Evaluation curves, computed with 6M visibility samples and measured using 160M evaluation samples.

Chapter 3. Algorithms for Scene Preprocessing

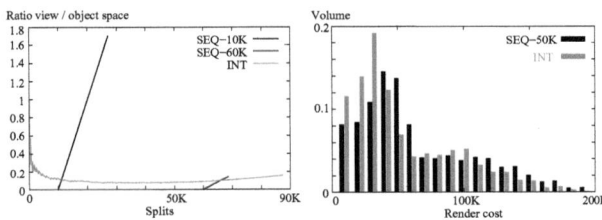

Figure 3.18: (left) Evaluation of the ratio of the total number of view cells and objects during the subdivision of Arena. (right) Histogram showing amount of view space volume in a particular range of render cost for the subdivision of Vienna.

space. We used different termination criteria of the initial object space subdivision (10k and 60k objects) to observe the dependence of the reference method on this parameter.

For both test scenes the subdivisions were constructed with 3M, and 6M visibility samples, respectively. We terminated the subdivisions when they reached a specified memory budget (35MB). After the construction of the subdivisions, we also evaluated the quality of the subdivision by casting a large number of visibility samples and recomputing the render cost and memory cost curves. We used 160M evaluation samples for both scenes. The results of these measurements are summarized in Figure 3.17. Our new method is labeled INT (interleaved) and the reference method is labeled SEQ (sequential) together with a number expressing the number of objects in the initial object space partition. We used a 2.2 GHz Dell Inspiron 9300 notebook with 2GB RAM for computing the results.

The middle and rightmost plots in Figure 3.17 show the evaluation of the subdivisions using 160M samples. We can see that the number of samples has significant influence on the results. Our method profits from increasing the number of samples from 3M to 6M in both scenes. On the other hand, the reference methods are sensitive to the larger number of samples only in Arena. It is hard to tell which would be the optimal number of samples for a certain scene. Our experiments indicate that with 6M samples, satisfactory results can be achieved for typical scenes such as the ones shown.

3.5. Optimized subdivisions for preprocessed visibility

Scene	Method	Time	Memory	View cells	Objects	Render cost	Speedup
Vienna	SEQ-10k	25 m	60 MB	11000	10000	81999.2	1.67
	SEQ-60k	21 m	60 MB	3000	60000	58149.2	1.18
	INT	212 m	60 MB	3106	60894	49221.9	–
Arena	SEQ-10k	33 m	80 MB	15500	10000	24631.4	2.53
	SEQ-60k	29 m	80 MB	5500	60000	12825.7	1.32
	INT	106 m	80 MB	5305	57195	9745.91	–

Table 3.2: Summary of results for Vienna and Arena scenes.

To analyze the behavior of the compared methods, we measured the ratio of the total number of view cells and objects during the subdivision process (Figure 3.18-(left)). This ratio is monotonically growing for the reference methods, whereas for the new method it adapts to the visibility properties of the scene. Interestingly, after a steady falloff the ratio increases again at the end of the subdivision.

The results show that with a sufficient number of visibility samples, the proposed method provides a consistent reduction of the average render cost at any given memory cost when compared to the reference methods. The render cost reductions for selected memory budgets are summarized in Table 3.2. Compared to the reference methods we obtained speedups of 16–68% for Vienna and 32–153% for Arena. Note that the speedup is based on the *average* render cost, a quantity which is smoothed over all view space, whereas locally the speedup can be much higher. For example, both scenes contain some large irreducible view cells which prevent large variations in the average render cost, therefore the speedups shown are quite significant. This fact is illustrated in Figure 3.18-(right), which depicts the histogram showing the distribution of render cost over the view space volume for Vienna. It can be seen that for the new method, significantly more volume is covered by lower render cost. We can see from Table 3.2 that our method requires several times more computation time than the sequential methods. However, to find a good subdivision using a sequential method, it would have to be evaluated several times for different numbers of objects, which would be even more costly. Most of the computation time of our method is spent evaluating

Chapter 3. Algorithms for Scene Preprocessing

Figure 3.19: Visualization of the view / object space partitions in the Vienna scene (left) and the Arena scene (right). Each colored patch represents one object from the PVS. We show a cut through the 3D view space subdivision. The view cells are colored from blue (low render cost) to magenta (high render cost).

local split planes for the view space splits, the cost of which highly depends on the number of visibility samples. A viable alternative is to use only mid splits, which speeds up computations a lot. Visualizations of the resulting subdivisions for both scenes can be seen in Figure 3.19.

3.6 Conclusions

In this chapter we discussed scene preprocessing into meaningful view cells and objects for subsequent PVS computations. We first gave a general overview of the properties of view space and object space, how they are connected and how this relates to visibility computations. Furthermore, we described our novel global view space sampling process which we use to collect the coarse visibility information that drives our algorithms.

Next we discussed our specific algorithms for solving two problems of this area. Both methods use a cost model in order to minimize the expected render cost of the resulting PVSs. The model is based on our global visibility estimation determined by sampling. The first algorithm deals with automatic view cell generation, and the second algorithm deals with a combined generation of optimal view space and object space partitions. The latter problem is much harder because of the interconnectivity of view and object

3.6. Conclusions

space regarding the render time and storage cost.

For the automatic view cell generation algorithm, we have shown that the method provides efficient sets of view cells for both indoor and outdoor environments. Since we use the actual visibility of the scene for driving the view cell construction, our view cells adapt to scene visibility changes. This is important for example for regions with no geometry, where other cell construction methods can fail. As a result of the view cell construction we obtain more than a fixed set of view cells. Depending on the properties of the visibility preprocessing algorithm or a runtime storage budget, we can extract a specified number of view cells which provide an optimized partition for a given granularity.

Then we have presented in detail our new tool which allows constructing an optimized subdivision of both view space and object space for preprocessed visibility. This method extends the previous algorithm by treating view space and object space partitioning together and progressively refining both subdivisions while minimizing the associated render and memory costs. Contrary to previous techniques, both subdivisions are driven by the actual visibility in the scene. This allows a better adaptation to the visibility distribution within the view space and the object space.

In the future we would like to improve our model of render cost. In particular we want to integrate the cost of state changes due to materials and textures in the algorithms. Further we want to deal with the issue of determining how many samples to use, by implementing an adaptive version that starts with a low number of samples and casts more samples on demand. We are also working on an algorithm which uses the scalability of the subdivisions for rapid sampling-based global visibility precomputation.

Chapter 3. Algorithms for Scene Preprocessing

> Our memory is our coherence,
> our reason, our feeling, even our
> action. Without it, we are nothing.
>
> Luis Buñuel

4

CHC++: Coherent Hierarchical Culling Revisited

In the previous chapter we discussed algorithms that prepare the scene for visibility preprocessing. In this chapter, we switch our topic to online occlusion culling, which requires zero preprocessing time, and can handle dynamic scenes. We present a new algorithm for efficient occlusion culling using hardware occlusion queries. The algorithm significantly improves on previous techniques by making better use of temporal and spatial coherence of visibility. This is achieved by using adaptive visibility prediction and query batching. As a result of the new optimizations, the number of issued occlusion queries and the number of rendering state changes are significantly reduced. We also propose a simple method for determining tighter bounding volumes for occlusion queries and a method which further reduces the pipeline stalls. The proposed method provides up to two or three times speedup over the previous state of the art. The new technique is simple to implement, does not rely on hardware calibration and integrates well with modern game engines.

4.1 Introduction

Occlusion culling is an important technique to reduce the time for rendering complex scenes. The availability of so-called hardware occlusion queries

Chapter 4. CHC++: Coherent Hierarchical Culling Revisited

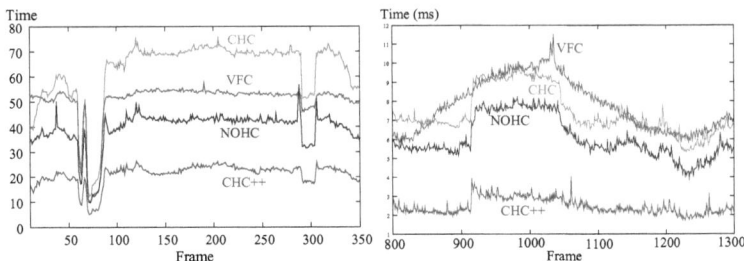

Figure 4.1: Frame time comparison for a walkthrough of the Powerplant model for View-Frustum Culling (VFC), Coherent Hierarchical Culling (CHC), Near Optimal Hierarchical Culling (NOHC), and our new algorithm (CHC++).

has made runtime determination of visibility attractive. Hardware occlusion queries are a mechanism by which graphics hardware can quickly report the visibility status of simple proxy geometry. However it was only by exploiting temporal coherence, e.g. in the Coherent Hierarchical Culling (CHC) algorithm [BWPP04], that using hardware occlusion queries became feasible, as this avoids CPU stalls and GPU starvation.

The CHC algorithm works well in densely occluded scenes, but the overhead of hardware occlusion queries makes it fall behind even simple view-frustum culling (VFC) in some situations. This was recognized by Guthe et al. [GBK06], who provide an algorithm, called Near Optimal Hierarchical Culling (NOHC), which reduces the number of queries based on a clever statistical model of occlusion and a hardware calibration step. However, it turns out that even the optimum defined by Guthe et al. can still be improved by exploiting further sources of simplification.

In this chapter, we propose CHC++, a method that significantly improves on previous online occlusion culling methods (see Figure 4.1). The core of the algorithm remains simple, requires no calibration, and allows easy integration into a game engine. The major contributions of the method are:

- **Reduction of state changes.** Despite its importance, the reduction of state changes was not explicitly addressed by previous occlusion

4.1. Introduction

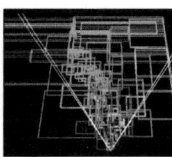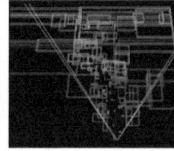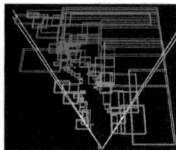

Figure 4.2: From left to right: (1) A sample view point in a city scene. (2) State changes required by the CHC algorithm (number of state changes = number of different colors of hierarchy nodes). (3) State changes required by the CHC++ algorithm. (4) Multiqueries: all invisible nodes are covered by only two occlusion queries (shown in different colors).

culling methods. Our method provides a powerful mechanism to minimize the number of state changes by using batching of queries. As a result the total number of state changes is reduced by more than an order of magnitude (see Figure 4.2).

- **Reduction of number of queries.** Reducing the number of queries was a major goal of previous research on hardware based occlusion culling. For example, the NOHC algorithm proposed by Guthe et al. [GBK06] is very successful at reducing the number of queries for views with low occlusion. We propose two new methods for further reduction of the number of queries. The first method resolves visibility of many nodes in the hierarchy by a single query, the second method exploits tighter bounding volumes for the queries without the need for any auxiliary data structures like oriented bounding boxes or k-dops. As a result we achieve a significantly lower number of queries than the "optimal" algorithm defined by Guthe et al. [GBK06] (see Figure 4.2).

- **Reduction of CPU stalls.** The CHC algorithm does a good job at reducing CPU stalls, however in certain scenarios stalls still occur and cause a performance penalty. We propose a simple modification which provides further reduction of the wait time, which at the same time integrates well with our method for reducing state changes.

- **Reduction of rendered geometry.** Tighter bounding volumes will

Chapter 4. CHC++: Coherent Hierarchical Culling Revisited

reduce the overestimation of visibility caused by bounding volumes and therefore reduce the amount of geometry classified as visible.

- **Integration with game engines.** Most game engines incorporate a highly optimized rendering loop in which sorting by materials and shaders is performed in order to minimize rendering state changes. Our method allows the rendering engine to perform such a sort on a batch of primitives stored in a render queue. Additionally the proposed technique significantly reduces the number of engine calls.

4.2 Overview

Since the CHC algorithm [BWPP04] and the NOHC algorithm [GBK06] are essential to our work on online occlusion culling, we review them and discuss some of their issues. Then we describe the major components of the new CHC++ algorithm.

4.2.1 CHC and its problems

The Coherent Hierarchical Culling algorithm [BWPP04] makes use of temporal and spatial coherence to reduce the overhead and latency of hardware occlusion queries. It traverses the hierarchy in a front-to-back order and issues queries only for previously visible leaves and nodes of the previously invisible boundary. Previously visible leaves are assumed to stay visible in the current frame, and hence they are rendered immediately. The result of the query for these nodes only updates their classification for the next frame. The invisible nodes are assumed to stay invisible, but the algorithm retrieves the query result in the current frame in order to discover visibility changes. Refer to Figure 4.6 for the pseudocode of the original original CHC algorithm (unmarked parts).

The reduction of the number of queries (queries are not issued on previously visible interior nodes) and clever interleaving reduced the overhead of occlusion queries to an acceptable quantity. The algorithm works very

4.2. Overview

well for scenarios that have a lot of occlusion. However, on newer hardware where rendering geometry becomes cheap compared to querying, or view points where much of the scene is visible, the method can become even slower than conventional view-frustum culling. This is a result of wasted queries and unnecessary state changes. This problem makes the CHC algorithm less attractive for game developers, who call for an algorithm which is reliably faster than view-frustum culling. Another problem of CHC lies in the complicated integration of the method into the rendering loop of highly optimized game engines. CHC interleaves rendering and querying of individual nodes of the spatial hierarchy, which does not allow the engine to perform material sorting and leads to a higher number of engine API calls.

4.2.2 NOHC and its problems

The Near Optimal Hierarchical Culling algorithm proposed by Guthe et al. [GBK06] tackles the problem of wasted queries. The method uses a calibrated model of graphics hardware to estimate costs of the queries and costs of rendering. It estimates occlusion of nodes by using a simple screen coverage model and further corrections assuming temporal coherence. The occlusion estimation and hardware model are used in a cost/benefit heuristics which decides whether to apply an occlusion query on the currently processed node. This heuristic uses a sophisticated reasonability test for queries with a couple of rules.

The algorithm saves a significant number of queries, especially queries which would be applied on visible nodes. This can lead to a significant improvement over the CHC algorithm if the "assumed visibility" optimization proposed for CHC is not used. This optimization assumes nodes to stay visible for a given number of frames, testing the nodes periodically according to that number and skipping the queries in between.

The results for NOHC indicate that with a proper hardware calibration, the method always performs better than view-frustum culling. In their paper, Guthe et al. [GBK06] also defined a theoretical optimal culling algorithm based on occlusion queries. The optimal algorithm is derived under the

Chapter 4. CHC++: Coherent Hierarchical Culling Revisited

assumption that the status of every invisible node has to be verified by an occlusion query. The NOHC method then closely approaches the optimal algorithm.

We show that the definition of optimality used by Guthe et al. [GBK06] still leaves significant room for improvement. In fact, the CHC++ algorithm is always clearly below the optimum defined by Guthe et al.

NOHC requires a hardware calibration step in which the hardware parameters are measured in a preprocess using artificial rendering scenarios. Measuring accurate parameters of the model requires very careful implementation. However, it turns out that even if precisely implemented, these measurements need not reflect the complex processes of state changes, pipelining, and interleaving rendering and occlusion queries during actual walkthroughs. Our new method does not rely on hardware calibration and aims to minimize its dependence on external parameters. In fact it leaves the user with loosely setting a few parameters whose influence is well predictable.

4.3 Our algorithm

4.3.1 Building blocks of CHC++

The new CHC++ algorithm method addresses all previously mentioned problems, and extends CHC by including the following new components:

Queues for batching of queries. Before a node is queried, it is appended to a queue. Separate queues are used for accumulating previously visible and previously invisible nodes. We use the queues to issue batches of queries instead of individual queries. This reduces state changes by one to two orders of magnitude. The batching of queries will be described in Section 4.3.2.

Multiqueries. We compile multiqueries (Section 4.3.3.1), which are able to cover more nodes by a single occlusion query. This reduces the number of queries for previously invisible nodes up to an order of magnitude.

Randomized sampling pattern for visible nodes. We apply a temporally jittered sampling pattern (Section 4.3.3.2) for scheduling queries for

4.3. Our algorithm

previously visible nodes. This reduces the number of queries for visible nodes and while spreading them evenly over the frames of the walkthrough.

Tight bounding volumes. We use tight bounding volumes (Section 4.3.4) without the need for their explicit construction. This provides a reduction of the number of rendered triangles as well as a reduction of the number of queries.

Previously frustum-culled nodes. The original CHC algorithm loses coherence if a node was previously view-frustum culled. This issue can be solved by using the original classification of a node *before* it was frustum culled (Section 4.3.5).

Note that for all tests presented in the paper we used an axis-aligned bounding volume hierarchy (BVH) constructed according to the surface area heuristics [MB90, Hav00]. The presented methods are however compatible with other types of spatial hierarchies [MBM*01], except for the tight bounding volumes optimization, which explicitly exploits the properties of BVH.

4.3.2 Reducing state changes

Changes of rendering state constitute a significant cost in the rendering pipeline. Previous occlusion culling methods focused mainly on scheduling the queries in a way that hides latencies and keeps the GPU occupied, as well as reducing the overall number of queries. However, even if the number of queries is reduced, every remaining query potentially leads to a state change in which at least writing to color and depth buffers is disabled and then re-enabled after the query. If complex shaders are used then this state change also involves switching the shader on and off.

It turns out that these changes of rendering state cause an even larger overhead than the query itself. The overhead may be on the hardware side (e.g., flushing caches), on the driver side or even on the application side. Thus it is highly desirable to reduce the number of state changes to an acceptable amount: game developers refer to about 200 state changes per frame as an acceptable value on current hardware.

Query batching. Our solution to this problem is based on batching

Chapter 4. CHC++: Coherent Hierarchical Culling Revisited

occlusion queries instead of issuing queries immediately when they are requested by the algorithm. The rendering state is changed only once per batch and thus the reduction of state changes directly corresponds to the size of the query batches we issue. The batching algorithm handles visible and invisible nodes differently as described in the following sections.

4.3.2.1 Batching previously invisible queries

The invisible nodes to be queried are appended to a queue which we call *i-queue*. When the number of nodes in the i-queue reaches a user-defined batch size b, we change the rendering state for querying and issue an occlusion query for each node in the i-queue (in Section 4.3.3.1 we will see how several nodes can be combined in one occlusion query in order to reduce the number of queries).

The batch size b is tightly connected with the reduction of render state changes, giving approximately b times less state changes than the CHC algorithm. On the other hand, batching effectively delays the availability of query results for invisible nodes, which means that visibility changes could be detected later and follow-up queries spawned by them would introduce further latency if there is not enough alternative work (e.g., rendering visible nodes) left.

An optimal value for b depends on the scene geometry, material shaders, and the capabilities of the rendering engine with respect to material sorting. For our scenes and rendering engine we observed that precise tuning of this parameter is not necessary and that values between 20 and 80 give a largely sufficient reduction of render state changes while not introducing additional latency into the method.

4.3.2.2 Batching previously visible queries

Recall that the CHC algorithm issues a query for each previously visible node and renders the geometry of the node without waiting for the result of the query. Similarly to CHC, our proposed method renders the geometry of previously visible nodes during the hierarchy traversal. However the queries

4.3. Our algorithm

are not issued immediately. Instead the corresponding nodes are stored in a queue which we call *v-queue*.

An important observation is that the queries for these nodes are not critical for the current frame since their result will only be used in the next frame. We exploit this observation by using nodes from the v-queue to fill up waiting time: whenever the traversal queue is empty and no outstanding query result is available, we process nodes from the v-queue.

As a result we perform adaptive batching of queries for previously visible nodes driven by the latency of the outstanding queries. At the end of the frame, when all queries for previously invisible nodes have been processed, the method just applies a single large batch for all unprocessed nodes from the v-queue.

Note that before processing a node from the v-queue, we also check whether a render state change is required. It turns out that in the vast majority of cases there is no need to change the render state at all as it was already changed by a previously issued query batch for invisible nodes. Therefore, we have basically eliminated state changes for previously visible nodes.

As a beneficial side effect, the v-queue reduces the effect of violations of the front-to-back ordering made by the original CHC algorithm. In particular if a previously hidden node occludes a previously visible node in the current frame, this effect would only be captured in the next frame, as the previously visible node would often be queried before the previously invisible node is rendered. This issue becomes apparent in situations where many visibility changes happen at the same time. Delaying the queries using the v-queue will make it more likely for such visibility changes to be detected.

The overview of the different queues used by the CHC++ algorithms is shown in Figure 4.3. Note that the overlaid nodes in the query queue correspond to multiqueries, which will be discussed in Section 4.3.3.1.

Chapter 4. CHC++: Coherent Hierarchical Culling Revisited

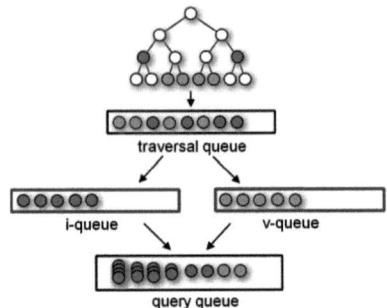

Figure 4.3: Different queues used by the CHC++ algorithm. The queues which were not used by the CHC algorithm are highlighted in blue.

4.3.2.3 Game engine integration

For easy integration of the CHC++ method into existing game engines we propose to use an additional queue in the algorithm which we call *render queue*. This queue accumulates all nodes scheduled for rendering and is processed when a batch of queries is about to be issued. When processing the render queue the engine can apply its internal material shader sorting and then render the objects stored in the queue in the new order. Another beneficial effect of the render queue is the reduction of engine API calls. These calls can be very costly and thus their reduction provides significant speedup as we experienced for example with the popular Ogre3D game engine [Jun06].

4.3.3 Reducing the number of queries

Recent online occlusion culling methods focused on reducing the number of occlusion queries in order to reduce their overhead. In particular the method of Guthe et al. [GBK06] proposed a sophisticated approach for eliminating queries based on a cost/benefit heuristics and a calibrated model of the graphics hardware. In this section we propose two new methods which are able to reduce the number of queries even *below* the hypothetical algorithm previously defined as optimal by Guthe et al.

4.3. Our algorithm

4.3.3.1 Multiqueries for invisible nodes

All previous techniques use one occlusion query per previously invisible primitive to be tested (node in a hierarchy, bounding volume, cell in a grid). The occlusion queries for these nodes were considered irreducible.

However, the following observation allows us to reduce the number of queries even for previously invisible nodes: If some previously invisible part of a scene remains invisible in the current frame, a single occlusion query for the whole part is sufficient to verify its visibility status. Such a query would render all bounding boxes of primitives in this scene part, and return zero if all primitives remain occluded. For example, in the extreme case of a static scene and a static view point, a single occlusion query could be used for all invisible parts of the scene.

Assuming a certain coherence of visibility, our new technique aims to identify such scene parts by forming groups of previously invisible nodes that are equally likely to remain invisible. A single occlusion query is issued for each such group, which we call a *multiquery*. If the multiquery returns zero visible fragments, all nodes in the group remain invisible and their status has been updated by the single query. Otherwise the coherence was broken for this group and we issue individual queries for all nodes by reinserting them in the i-queue. Note that in the first case the number of queries is reduced by the number of primitives in the group. However, in the second case the multiquery for the batch was wasted.

We use an adaptive mechanism based on a cost/benefit heuristics to find suitable node groupings. The crucial part of the evaluation is the estimation of coherence in the visibility classification of the nodes, which is described in the next section. The actual heuristics will be described in Section 4.3.3.1.

The multiqueries provide another step towards output sensitivity of the algorithm: large static invisible parts of the scene are culled very quickly and most of the effort is spent on the parts of the scene that are visible or frequently change their visibility classification.

Chapter 4. CHC++: Coherent Hierarchical Culling Revisited

Estimating coherence of visibility In the vast majority of cases there is a strong coherence in visibility for most nodes in the hierarchy. Our aim is to quantify this coherence. In particular, knowing the visibility classification of a given node, we aim to estimate the probability that this node will keep its visibility classification in the next frame. Our experiments indicate that there is a strong correlation of this value with the "history" of the node, i.e., with the number of frames the node already kept the same visibility classification (we call this value *visibility persistence*). Nodes that have been invisible for a very long time are likely to stay invisible. Such nodes could be the engine block of a car, for example, that will never be visible unless the camera moves inside of the car engine. On the contrary, even in slow moving scenarios, there are always some nodes on the visible border which frequently change their classification. Hence there is a quite high chance for nodes that recently became invisible to become visible soon.

We define the desired probability as a function of the visibility persistence i, and approximate it based on the history of previous nodes:

$$p_{keep}(i) \approx \frac{n_i^{keep}}{n_i^{all}}, \qquad (4.1)$$

where n_i^{keep} is the number of already tested nodes which have been in the same state for i frames and keep their state in the $i+1$-th frame, and n_i^{all} is the total number of already tested nodes which have been in the same state for i frames. Figure 4.4 shows a plot of the probability p_{keep} against the visibility persistence i. The counters n_i^{keep} and n_i^{all} are accumulated over all previous frames of the walkthrough.

In the first few frames there are not enough measurements for accurate computation of $p_{keep}(i)$, especially for larger values of i. We solve this problem by piecewise constant propagation of the already computed values to the higher values of $p_{keep}(i)$.

As a simpler alternative to evaluating $p_{keep}(i)$ by measurements, we propose an analytic formula which corresponds reasonably well to the functions we measured for our scenes and walkthroughs:

4.3. Our algorithm

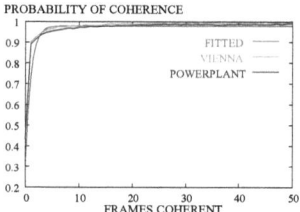

Figure 4.4: $p_{keep}(i)$ in dependence on visibility persistence i. Note that the analytic function from Eq. 4.2 closely matches the functions measured for Powerplant and Vienna scenes.

$$p_{keep}(i) \approx 0.99 - 0.7e^{-i}. \qquad (4.2)$$

Using this function does not provide as accurate estimations of p_{keep} as the measured function, but can be used to avoid implementing the evaluation of the measured function. Figure 4.4 illustrates the analytic function and the measured functions for two different scenes.

Cost/benefit model for multiqueries Determining the optimal size of a multiquery for previously invisible nodes in a given batch (i.e., the i-queue) is a global optimization problem that requires evaluation of all possible partitions of the batch into multiqueries. Instead, we use a greedy model which maximizes a benefit/cost ratio for each multiquery.

The cost is the expected number of queries issued per one multiquery, which is expressed as:

$$C(M) = 1 + p_{fail}(M) * |M|, \qquad (4.3)$$

where $p_{fail}(M)$ is the probability that the multiquery fails (returns visible, in which case all nodes have to be tested individually) and $|M|$ is the number of nodes in the multiquery. Note that the constant 1 represents the cost of the multiquery itself, whereas $p_{fail}(M) * |M|$ expresses the expected number of additionally issued queries for individual nodes. The probability p_{fail} is calculated from the visibility persistence values i_N of nodes in the multiquery

Chapter 4. CHC++: Coherent Hierarchical Culling Revisited

as:

$$p_{fail}(M) = 1 - \prod_{\forall N \in M} p_{keep}(i_N). \tag{4.4}$$

The benefit of the multiquery is simply the number of nodes in the multiquery, i.e. $B(M) = |M|$.

Given the nodes in the i-queue, the greedy optimization algorithm maximizes the benefit at the given cost. We first sort the nodes in descending order based on their probability of staying invisible, i.e. $p_{keep}(i_N)$. Then, starting with the first node in the queue, we add the nodes to the multiquery and at each step we evaluate the value V of the multiquery as a benefit/cost ratio:

$$V(M_j) = \frac{B(M_j)}{C(M_j)}. \tag{4.5}$$

It turns out that V reaches a maximum for a particular M_j and thus j corresponds to the optimal size of the multiquery for the nodes in the front of the i-queue. Once we find this maximum, we issue the multiquery for the corresponding nodes and repeat the process until the i-queue is used up. As a result we compile larger multiqueries for nodes with high probability of staying invisible and small multiqueries for nodes which are likely to turn visible.

4.3.3.2 Skipping tests of visible nodes

The original CHC algorithm introduced an important optimization in order to reduce the number of queries on previously visible nodes. A visible node is assumed to stay visible for n_{av} frames and it will only be tested in the frame $n_{av} + 1$. This optimization effectively reduces the average number of queries for previously visible leaves by a factor of $n_{av} + 1$.

This simple method however has a problem that the queries can be temporally aligned. This query alignment becomes problematic in situations when nodes tend to become visible in the same frame. For example consider the case when the view point moves from the ground level above the roof

4.3. Our algorithm

level in a typical city scene, causing many nodes to become visible in the same frame. Afterwards the queries of those nodes will be scheduled for the $n_{av} + 1$-th frame, and thus most of the queries will be aligned again. The average number of queries per frame will still be reduced, but the alignment can cause observable frame rate drops.

We observed that a randomization of $n_{av} + 1$ by a small random value $-r_{max} < r < r_{max}$ does not solve the problem in a satisfying manner. The problem is that if the randomization is small, the queries might still be very much aligned. On the other hand, if the randomization is big, some of the queries will be processed too late and thus the change from visible to invisible state will be captured too late.

We found that the most satisfying solution is achieved by randomizing the *first invocation* of the occlusion query. After a node has turned visible, we use a random value $0 < r < n_{av}$ for determining the next frame when a query will be issued. Subsequently, if the node was already visible in the previous test, we use a regular sampling interval given by n_{av}.

We experimented with various values of n_{av}. The optimal value depends on the scene itself, inspection coherence, hardware parameters as well as the rendering engine parameters. Fortunately, our tests show that the dependence is not very strong and a value of $5 - 10$ has been a safe and robust choice for all tests.

4.3.4 Tight bounding volumes

Apart from the overhead introduced by occlusion queries, the success of a culling algorithm depends strongly on how tightly the bounding volumes in the spatial hierarchy approximate the contained geometry. If the fit is not tight enough, many nodes will be classified as visible even though the contained geometry is not. There are several techniques for obtaining tight bounding volumes, mostly by replacing axis- aligned bounding boxes by more complex shapes. While these methods could directly be applied to most occlusion culling algorithms, they also constitute an overhead of calculating and maintaining these volumes. This can become costly especially for dynamic

Chapter 4. CHC++: Coherent Hierarchical Culling Revisited

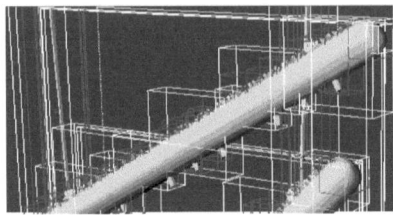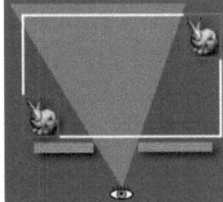

Figure 4.5: Tight bounding volumes for nodes of the BVH which more closely represent the objects shown as spheres. The tight bounding volume consists of bounding boxes of the children (red) instead of the parent box (white).

scenes.

We propose a simple method for determining tight bounds for *inner nodes* in the context of hardware occlusion queries applied to an arbitrary bounding volume hierarchy. For a particular node we determine its *tight bounding volume* as a collection of bounding volumes of its children at a particular depth (see Figure 4.5).

It turns out that when using up-to-date APIs for rendering the bounding volume geometry (e.g., OpenGL vertex buffer objects), a slightly more complex geometry for the occlusion query practically does not increase its overhead. However, there might be a penalty for rasterizing the tight bounding volumes when some of the smaller bounding primitives overlap in screen space, thus increasing the fill rate compared to projecting the original bounding volume of the node. To avoid such a case, we use a simple test to ensure the usefulness of the tight bounds. When collecting the child nodes for the tight bounding volume, we test if the sum of surface areas of the bounding volumes of the children is not larger than s_{max} times the surface area of the parent node (note that this does not depend on a particular view point). If this is the case, we terminate traversal and do not further refine the bounding representation. We terminate the search for bounding volumes if the depth from the node is greater than a specified maximal depth d_{max}. The following values gave good results in our tests: $d_{max} = 3$, $s_{max} = 1.4$.

Note that it is advantageous to determine the tight bounding volumes

4.3. Our algorithm

also for *leaves* of the hierarchy. This can be easily achieved by building a slightly deeper hierarchy and then marking interior nodes of the hierarchy containing less than a specified number of triangles as *virtual leaves*, i.e., interior nodes that are considered as leaves during traversal.

As a result, tight bounding volumes provide several benefits at almost no cost: (1) earlier culling of interior nodes of the hierarchy, (2) culling of leaves which would otherwise be classified as visible, (3) increase of coherence of visibility classification of interior nodes. The first property leads to a reduction of the number of queries. The second property provides a reduction of the number of rendered triangles. Finally, the third benefit avoids changes in visibility classification for interior nodes caused by repeated pull-up and pull-down of visibility.

4.3.5 Previously frustum-culled nodes

We always classify previously frustum-culled nodes as invisible in the original CHC algorithm, hence coherence is lost for these nodes. This can be problematic in situations with quick rotations of the viewer, and can lead to frame rate drops. It is not beneficial to treat all the previously frustum-culled nodes as visible either. We propose to keep the visibility classification of the nodes *before* it was frustum culled, assuming that the visibility status of the nodes has not changed if no further information is available. If a node has been part of an invisible subtree we classify it as invisible. Likewise, we handle the case that a node has been visible.

This method requires to store an additional *previously frustum culled* flag to indicate if a node has newly entered the view frustum in the current frame. Furthermore, as this flag is only set for the root node of a frustum-culled subtree, the information has to be passed down the subtree to the leaves during traversal. Note that we did not include this extension in the pseudocode in Figure 4.6 because it would make the essence of the algorithm harder to understand.

Chapter 4. CHC++: Coherent Hierarchical Culling Revisited

```
CHC++ begin
    DistanceQueue.push(Root);
    while !DistanceQueue.Empty() || !QueryQueue.Empty() do
        while !QueryQueue.Empty() && (DistanceQueue.Empty() ||
        FirstQueryFinished) do
++          while !FirstQueryFinished && !v-queue.Empty() do
++              IssueQuery(v-queue.pop());
++          N = QueryQueue.Pop();
++          HandleReturnedQuery(N);
        else if !DistanceQueue.Empty() then
            N = DistanceQueue.DeQueue();
            N.IsVisible = false; // invisible by default
            if InsideViewFrustum(N) then
                if !WasVisible(N) then
                    QueryPreviouslyInvisibleNode(N);
                else
                    if N.IsLeaf() then
                        if QueryReasonable(N) then
                            v-queue.push(N);
                        else
                            PullUpVisibility(N)
                    TraverseNode(N);

++      if DistanceQueue.Empty() then
++          // issue remaining query batch
++          IssueMultiQueries();

++  while !v-queue.empty() do
++      // remaining prev. visible node queries
++      IssueQuery(v-queue.pop());
++  while !QueryQueue.empty() do
++      N = QueryQueue.pop();
++      HandleReturnedQuery(N);
end
```

Figure 4.6: Pseudo-code of the CHC++ main traversal loop. The differences to the original CHC are marked in blue.

4.3. Our algorithm

```
TraverseNode(N) begin
    if IsLeaf(N) then
     | Render(N);
    else
        DistanceQueue.PushChildren(N);
        N.IsVisible = false;
end
PullUpVisibility(N) begin
    while !N.IsVisible do
     | N.IsVisible = true; N = N.Parent;
end
HandleReturnedQuery(Q) begin
    if Q.visiblePixels > threshold then
++       if Q.size() > 1 then
++        | QueryInvididualNodes(Q); // failed multiquery
        else
            if !WasVisible(N) then
             | TraverseNode(N);
            PullUpVisibility(N);
    else
     | N.IsVisible = false;
end
++ QueryPreviouslyInvisibleNode(N) begin
++     i-queue.push(N) ;
++     if i-queue.size() ≥ maxPrevInvisNodesBatchSize then
++      | IssueMultiQueries(); // issue the query batch
++ end
++ IssueMultiQueries() begin
++     while !i-queue.Empty() do
++         MQ = i-queue.GetNextMultiQuery();
++         IssueQuery(MQ); i-queue.PopNodes(MQ);
++
end
```

Figure 4.7: Pseudo-code of selected important functions. The differences to the original CHC are marked in blue.

Chapter 4. CHC++: Coherent Hierarchical Culling Revisited

4.3.6 Putting it all together

The CHC++ algorithm aims to keep the simplicity of the CHC algorithm, with several important add-ons. In this section we summarize the complete CHC++ algorithm and emphasize its main differences from the CHC algorithm. The pseudocode of the CHC++ algorithm is shown in Figure 4.6.

As in CHC, we use a priority queue for traversing the hierarchy. This queue provides a front-to-back order of the processed nodes. Unlike CHC, the new algorithm uses two new queues for storing nodes which should be queried (v-queue and i-queue). These two queues are the key for reduction of rendering state changes and compiling multiqueries.

The previously visible nodes are rendered immediately as for CHC. If they are scheduled for testing in the current frame, they are placed in the v-queue. The algorithm for scheduling the queries uses the discussed temporally jittered sampling pattern to reduce the number of queries and to distribute them evenly over frames. The queries for nodes stored in the v-queue are used to fill up the wait time if it should occur. At the end of the frame the remaining nodes in the v-queue form a single batch of queries.

The i-queue accumulates processed nodes which have been invisible in the previous frames. When there is a sufficient number of nodes in the queue, we apply a batch of occlusion queries for nodes in the i-queue while compiling them into the multiqueries.

When integrating the method into a game engine, the visible nodes are first accumulated in a render queue. The render queue is then processed by the engine before a batch of queries from i-queue is about to be issued.

4.3.6.1 Handling dynamic objects

In our implementation we handle dynamic objects by generating two separate BVH hierarchies over the same scene, one for the static geometry that is optimized with the powerful *surface area heuristic* (described in Section 2.2.7), the other one for the dynamic objects using a simple *spatial median split* heuristics that is quick to evaluate. Both hierarchies are parented under a common root node, hence it is completely transparent to any traversal algo-

4.4. Results

Vienna	Pompeii	Powerplant
2,583,674 triangles	5,646,041 triangles	12,748,510 triangles
18,264 objects	44,913 objects	19,528 objects
10,535 BVH nodes	22,468 BVH nodes	17,793 BVH nodes

Table 4.1: Statistics for all scenes.

rithm that there initially have been two hierarchies. Each frame we rebuild the dynamic branch of the hierarchy from scratch. Therefore we remember the visibility classification of each object from the last frame, and use them to reconstruct the visibility classifications of the new hierarchy nodes by pulling up the classification of previously invisible nodes. This method is sufficiently efficient if the number of dynamic objects is reasonably low, e.g., in the range of some hundred dynamic objects.

For a larger number of dynamic objects, this rather brute force method could become inefficient. In this case we suggest the following strategy: upon change we just enlarge the bounding volumes of the dynamic hierarchy starting from the bounding boxes of the leaves in a bottom up fashion (which is a fast operation), so that they always fully contain the geometry. If the ratio between the area of the bounding volume and the area of the bounding box of the containing geometry becomes too large (i.e., the culling becomes too conservative), the corresponding geometry is reinserted into the hierarchy. To prevent situations where too many objects are reinserted in the same frame, we can use a lazy update: only the n worst objects in terms of the aforementioned criterion are updated in a single frame.

Chapter 4. CHC++: Coherent Hierarchical Culling Revisited

parameter name	value
assumed visible frames	10
previously invisible nodes batch size	50
depth for testing children	3
maximal depth for tight bounds	3
maximal surface ratio for tight bounds	1.4

Table 4.2: Parameters for CHC++.

4.4 Results

For all our results we used an Intel Quad Core 2.66 MHz CPU and an NVidia 8800 GTX graphics card. We tested our method on three different scenes: Vienna, a typical city scene with detailed street objects and trees (2,583,674 triangles and 10,535 BVH nodes); Pompeii, a generated city scene with detailed buildings (5,646,041 triangles and 22,468 BVH nodes), and the Powerplant model (12,748,510 triangles and 17,793 BVH nodes) (refer to Table 4.1). In all plots we consistently use the following abbreviations: VFC for View-Frustum Culling, CHC for Coherent Hierarchical Culling, NOHC for Near Optimal Hierarchical Culling, and CHC++ for our new method. We used the parameters listed in Table 4.2 for all our measurements of CHC++. These parameters have been quite optimal for all of our tests.

On a different hardware it may be necessary to adjust these parameters for reaching optimal performance, which can be achieved with a simple tool that measures the optimal values once for each target platform by sampling a number of view points or pieces of walkthrough. While it pays off to have large queues on modern PC hardware where the penalty for state changes is high, it may not be so for consoles that have a lot of potential for optimizing different parts of the rendering process and hence also the occlusion queries.

Figure 4.1, shown in the beginning of the paper, presents a frame time comparison for a walkthrough in the Powerplant. It can be seen that the CHC algorithm performs worse than view-frustum culling for some parts of the walkthrough. While NOHC is at least not worse than view-frustum culling, our algorithm performs up to two times better than NOHC.

Figure 4.8 shows the frame times in a walkthrough in Pompeii and studies

4.4. Results

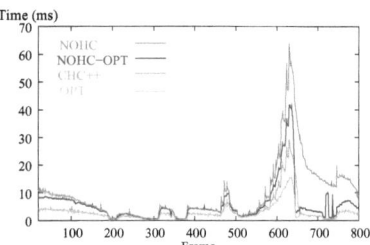

Figure 4.8: Frame time comparison of NOHC, the optimal algorithm as defined by Guthe et al. (OPT-NOHC), CHC++, and an algorithm that renders only visible nodes without querying (OPT) in the Pompeii scene.

the behavior with respect to NOHC and two artificial reference algorithms (NOHC-OPT and OPT). The NOHC-OPT method refers to the function defined as optimum by Guthe et al. [GBK06], which issues queries for all invisible nodes but only if they are feasible according to their cost model. The OPT method refers to an hypothetical algorithm that will only render the visible nodes of the hierarchy without issuing any query. OPT therefore does not depend on the cost or implementation of occlusion queries at all and is the fastest solution that can be achieved with a given hierarchy. We implemented the OPT method by recording the visibility results using the exact stop-and-wait algorithm, which does not make use of temporal coherence, and then timing the frame rerendering it again with the already computed visibility classification.

As claimed by the authors, NOHC is very close to the NOHC-OPT algorithm, except for difficult view points with a lot of visible geometry. More notably, CHC++ is clearly significantly faster than NOHC-OPT practically everywhere. Furthermore, CHC++ is approaching the OPT curve for the moderately complex parts of the scene, which is remarkable since OPT cannot be beaten by any algorithm using occlusion queries on the given hierarchy.

There is still some noticeable overhead of CHC++ compared to OPT in the high frame time parts of the walkthrough, which correspond to views from over the buildings where a lot of the scene becomes visible and where

Chapter 4. CHC++: Coherent Hierarchical Culling Revisited

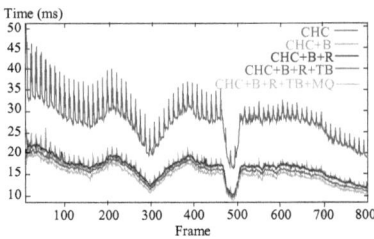

Figure 4.9: The benefit of different optimizations in a walkthrough of the Powerplant. We start with CHC and add one optimization at a time. The bottom curve with all optimizations corresponds to CHC++. The abbreviations have the following meaning: B = batching of previously visible and invisible nodes, R = randomization, TB = tight bounds, MQ = multiqueries.

we have to issue many queries to capture the changes in visibility. The rest of the time difference is caused by an accumulation of minor things, like the overhead for maintaining all the queues.

Figure 4.9 shows the benefit of each optimization individually in another walkthrough in the Powerplant. It is clearly visible that the batching brings the majority of the benefit. Query batching already removes a lot of the query overhead, otherwise the benefit of some of the other optimizations would be much more prominent. The randomization is most important in situations when many nodes become visible at once, which is well visible in the beginning of the walkthrough. The benefit of multiqueries depends on the absolute number of previously invisible nodes, which in turn depends on the properties of the hierarchy (a deeper hierarchy would mean more benefit from multiqueries). Note that the relative benefits of the different optimizations can change for different hardware architectures and rendering engines.

In Figure 4.10 we study how CHC++ and NOHC behave on a walkthrough in the Powerplant with respect to *shader complexity*. We made three different tests: In the first test we used a depth only pass (DP), in the second test we used the standard fixed pipeline material shading of the original Powerplant model (FIX). In the third test we applied a moderately complex shader to all renderable geometry (i.e., the shader has 40 texture

4.4. Results

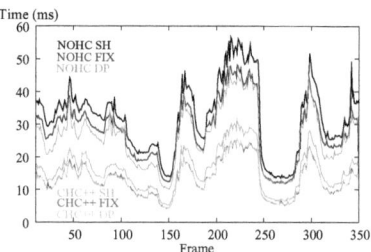

Figure 4.10: Dependence of the frame time on shader complexity in a walkthrough in the Powerplant. DP refers to depth only pass, FIX to fixed pipeline shading only, SH to a shader of moderately high complexity.

lookups).

Note that the used walkthrough is challenging for methods that exploit coherence because it has many swift changes in visibility. As can be seen, the dependence on the shader complexity is very low for CHC++. NOHC shows a much stronger dependence, performing visibly better for the depth pass than for the shaded geometry. Still the depth pass is much slower than for CHC++. Obviously the state changes lower the performance for the depth-only pass as well, even if it only involves a switch of the depth write flag.

Figure 4.11 analyzes the behavior of all methods in the Vienna scene, particularly with respect to the number of *queries and state changes*. This figure shows that CHC++ fulfills the claim that it significantly reduces both queries and state changes, and that this also translates into a significant performance advantage over the other algorithms.

Figure 4.12, left, shows the dependence of the frame time (averaged over several hundred frames) on the size of the batches for previously invisible nodes. We took measurements for batch sizes 10, 30, 50, 100, 200, and 300. We can observe that the method performs very stable for a wide range of batch sizes. However note that on older hardware large batch sizes of 100 and higher might cause a more prominent delay, because of longer wait time until a query returns.

Chapter 4. CHC++: Coherent Hierarchical Culling Revisited

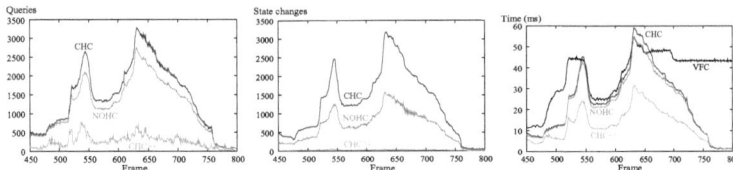

Figure 4.11: Comparison of issued queries (left), state changes (middle), and the resulting frame rates for a walkthrough in Vienna. Note that VFC does not impose any additional state changes.

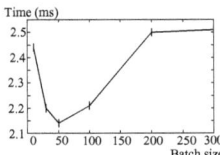

Figure 4.12: Dependence of the average frame time on the query batch size in a walkthrough in the Powerplant scene.

The effect of our new treatment of frustum-culled nodes can be seen in Figure 4.13. The figure shows swift turns in the Powerplant scene where the Powerplant quickly enters / leaves the view frustum. For the previous classification (OLD VFC) we can observe frame rate drops resulting from lost coherence, as compared to the new method (NEW VFC) that does not show this behavior.

4.5 Conclusions

We proposed several modifications to the CHC algorithm [BWPP04]. These modifications provide a significant reduction of state changes, number of queries, rendered triangles, and a further reduction of pipeline stalls. These benefits are achieved by batching of occlusion queries, multiqueries which cover more nodes with a single query, a randomly jittered temporal sampling pattern for queries, and tight bounding volumes.

The results show that compared to previous methods, the new method

4.5. Conclusions

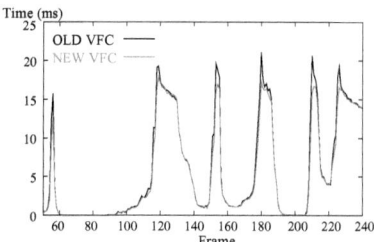

Figure 4.13: Sequence from the Powerplant showing swift turns of the view point. The old classification of previously view frustum culled nodes (OLD VFC) suffers from frame rate drops which do not happen for the new classification (NEW VFC).

provides up to two orders of magnitude reduction in the number of state changes and up to one order of magnitude reduction in the number of queries. These savings translate into a twofold speedup compared to CHC and about 1.5x speedup compared to NOHC [GBK06]. The proposed method is for most cases within a few percent of the "ideal" method which would know visibility classification in advance and render visible geometry only without using any occlusion queries. We believe that the new algorithm will become useful for game programmers as it is stable, easy to implement, and it integrates well with game engines.

In the future we want to study the possibility of automatic parameter adaptation during the walkthrough by exploiting the dependence of the total frame time on the number of issued queries and rendered triangles.

Chapter 4. CHC++: Coherent Hierarchical Culling Revisited

Where there is much light, the shadow is deep.

Johann Wolfgang von Goethe

5

High Quality Screen-Space Ambient Occlusion using Temporal Coherence

In this chapter we will further exploit temporal coherence for visibility computations. This time the topic is not qualitative visibility in the form of binary visibility culling for rendering acceleration – instead we investigate quantitative visibility. In particular we improve the quality and speed of an advanced shading technique called ambient occlusion, which is a cheap but effective approximation of global illumination, in screen space. Screen-space ambient occlusion (SSAO) methods sample the frame buffer as a discretization of the scene geometry, which makes the cost of the shading technique practically independent of the scene size - a very useful property to achieve output-sensitive rendering in real time. We present Temporal SSAO (TSSAO), a fast new SSAO algorithm which produces high-quality ambient occlusion without either noise or blurring artifacts, even for geometry with fine-grained high-frequency structures. Our algorithm exploits temporal coherence to cache and reuse previously computed SSAO samples, and adaptively applies more samples and spatial filtering only in regions that do not yet have enough information available from previous frames. The method works well for both static and dynamic scenes. Combined with our CHC++ algorithm, we are able to render large dynamic scenes with plausible indirect

Chapter 5. High Quality Screen-Space Ambient Occlusion using Temporal Coherence

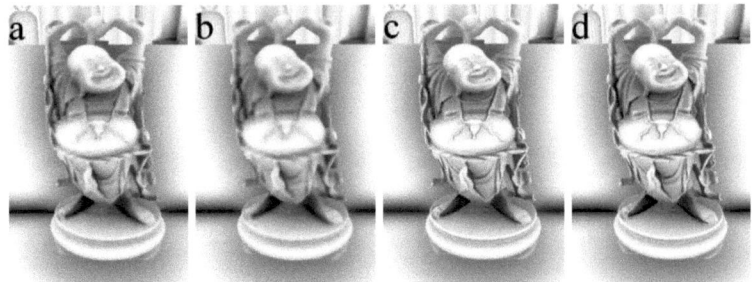

Figure 5.1: From left to right: SSAO without temporal coherence (23 FPS) with 32 samples per pixel, with (a) a weak blur, (b) a strong blur. (c) TSSAO (45 FPS), using 8–32 samples per pixel (initially 32, 8 in a converged state). (d) Reference solution using 480 samples per frame (2.5 FPS). All images at 1024x768 resolution. The scene has 7M vertices and runs at 62 FPS without SSAO shading.

illumination in real time.

5.1 Introduction

Ambient occlusion (as defined in Section 2.5.3) is heavily used in production rendering and recently also in real-time rendering and many high-profile games [Mit07, FM08], because it is a *local* effect (due to the limited sampling radius) that is very cheap compared to full global illumination, but still greatly enhances the perceived realism of the scene. Figure 5.2 demonstrates the visual impact of ambient occlusion. SSAO techniques decouple the shading from the scene complexity by using the frame buffer as a discrete approximation of the scene geometry. The performance of SSAO depends mainly on the number of samples per frame, hence a relatively small number of samples is typically used to reach the desired performance, and the resulting noise is blurred with a spatial depth-aware filter. However, a small number of samples can be insufficient for shading complex geometry with fine details, especially if a large sampling radius is used. The final image will look either noisy or blurry, depending on the size of the filter kernel. Gener-

5.1. Introduction

Figure 5.2: This figure compares rendering without (left) and with (right) ambient occlusion, and shows that AO allows much better depth perception and feature recognition, without requiring any additional lighting.

ally a careful tuning of the filter parameters is required in order to provide stable results, otherwise artifacts may appear, e.g., halos around small depth discontinuities.

In this paper, we present an algorithm that achieves high-quality ambient occlusion which is neither blurry nor prone to noise artifacts, with a minimum amount of samples per frame. We reuse the available AO information from previous frames by exploiting temporal coherence between consecutive image frames. We identify pixels describing identical world positions by means of temporal reprojection. The current state of the solution is cached in a so-called *ambient occlusion buffer*. Each frame we compute a few new AO samples, then blend these with the accumulated samples from the previous frames. The ambient occlusion solution is then combined with the image resulting from direct diffuse illumination in a separate step. See Figure 5.1 for a comparison of SSAO with and without employing temporal coherence.

Reprojection techniques have been used for a number of different tasks in the last couple of years, like antialiasing or shadow mapping. SSAO is an especially interesting case because it takes a pixel neighborhood into account, which leads to unique challenges, especially for dynamic scenes. First, since SSAO is a postprocessing operation, information about reprojection needs to be stored during the main rendering pass. Second, the validity of reprojected pixels does not depend only on the pixel itself, but also on its neighborhood,

Chapter 5. High Quality Screen-Space Ambient Occlusion using Temporal Coherence

requiring a new validity test for reprojected pixels. Third, the convergence of the solution allows us to reduce or completely omit spatial filtering that is typically necessary in SSAO methods, and allows us to rely on a minimal number of new samples per frame. For pixels that have not converged, e.g., when cached samples have been invalidated, we can use information about convergence in order to reconstruct the value from nearby samples using an adaptive convergence-aware filter that gives more weight to already converged samples.

5.2 Our algorithm

Ambient occlusion [CT81] evaluates the reverse surface exposure, and is computed by integrating the visibility function over all directions Ω on the hemisphere:

$$\text{AO}(p) = \frac{1}{\pi} \int_\Omega V(p, \omega')(n \cdot \omega') d\omega', \tag{5.1}$$

for a surface point p with normal n and a (inverse) binary visibility function V.

$$V(p, \omega') = \begin{cases} 0 & \text{if direction } \omega' \text{ is blocked} \\ 1, & \text{otherwise.} \end{cases} \tag{5.2}$$

In practice we consider occluders within a certain sampling radius only, or we use a non-binary visibility function that provides a smooth falloff for increasing distance to the surface point.

5.2.1 SSAO generation

SSAO methods aim to approximate the original AO integral in screen space. Several versions of SSAO with different assumptions and trade-offs have been described [BSD08, Mit07, RGS09]. While we demonstrated our technique only with two different ambient occlusion methods it works with many more,

5.2. Our algorithm

and could be used for several other shading method that depend on a screen-space sampling kernel. We assume that such a shading method can be written as an average over contributions C which depend on a series of samples s_i:

$$AO_n(p) = \frac{1}{n}\sum_{i=1}^{n} C(p, s_i) \quad (5.3)$$

A typical example contribution function for SSAO would be

$$C(p, s_i) = V(p, s_i)\max(\cos(s_i - p, n_p), 0)$$

where $V(p, s_i)$ is a binary visibility function that gives 0 if s_i is visible from p and 1 otherwise. Visibility is for example determined by checking whether s_i is visible in the z-buffer, and sometimes attenuated with the distance from p. We assume that the samples s_i have been precomputed and stored in a texture, for example a set of 3D points uniformly distributed in the hemisphere, which are transformed into the tangent space of p for the evaluation of C. For faster convergence we use a Halton sequence for sample generation, which is known for its low discrepancy [WH00].

5.2.2 Reprojection

Reprojection techniques use two render targets in ping-pong fashion, one for the current frame and one representing the cached information from the previous frames (denoted as *real-time reprojection cache* [NSL*07] or *history buffer [SJW07]*). In our context we cache ambient occlusion values and therefore denote this buffer as *ambient occlusion buffer*.

For static geometry, reprojection is constant for the whole frame, and can be carried out in the pixel shader or in a separate shading pass (in the case of deferred shading) using the following formula, where t denotes the post-perspective position of a pixel [SJW07]:

$$t_{prev_{x',y',z'}} = P_{prev}V_{prev}V^{-1}P^{-1}t_{x,y,z} \quad (5.4)$$

In our deferred shading pipeline, we store eye linear depth values for the new and the old frame, and use them to reconstruct the world space positions

Chapter 5. High Quality Screen-Space Ambient Occlusion using Temporal Coherence

Figure 5.3: The frame-to-frame optical flow using color coding for a rotating Happy Buddha. The fixpoint of the rotation is visible as a dark spot.

p. Note that p_{prev} can be obtained from the above formula by applying the inverse view-projection matrix to t. For dynamic scenes, this simple formula does not work because reprojection depends on the transformations of moving objects. Nehab et al. [NSL*07] therefore propose to do the reprojection in the vertex shader by applying the complete vertex transformation twice, once using the current transformation parameters (modeling matrix, skinning etc.) and once using the parameters of the previous frame.

However, in a deferred shading pipeline, p_{prev} needs to be accessed in a separate shading pass, where information about transformation parameters is already lost. Therefore, we store the 3D optical flow $p_{prev} - p$ in the frame buffer as another shading parameter (alongside normal, material etc.), using a lower precision than for the absolute depth values (16 bit vs. 32 bit). See Figure 5.3 for a depiction of optical flow induced by a rotating Happy Buddha model.

During reprojection, we have to check for pixels that became *invalid* (e.g. due to a disocclusion). This will be described in Section 5.2.4, where we also show that SSAO imposes some additional constraints for a pixel to stay valid.

5.2.3 Temporal refinement

The main idea of our algorithm is to spread the computation of ambient occlusion (Equation 5.3) over several frames by using reprojection. Whenever possible we take the solution from the old frame that corresponds to an image

5.2. Our algorithm

pixel and refine it with the contribution of new samples computed in the current frame. In frame $t+1$, we calculate a new contribution C_{t+1} from k new samples:

$$C_{t+1}(p) = \frac{1}{k} \sum_{i=n_t(p)+1}^{n_t(p)+k} C(p, s_i) \qquad (5.5)$$

and combine them with the previously computed solution from frame t:

$$AO_{t+1}(p) = \frac{n_t(p) AO_t(p_{prev}) + k C_{t+1}(p)}{n_t(p) + k} \qquad (5.6)$$

$$n_{t+1}(p) = min(n_t(p) + k, n_{max}) \qquad (5.7)$$

n_t keeps track of the number of samples that are have been accumulated yet in the solution. n_t is stored in a separate channel in the ambient occlusion buffer. We also store the starting index into the set of precomputed samples, which is used to take the new sampling positions for the current frame from a precomputed low-discrepancy Halton sequence. If the cached AO value is invalid, then n_t is simply set to 0. Otherwise, the solution will reach a stable state after a few frames.

Theoretically, this approach can use arbitrarily many samples. In practice, however, this is not advisable: since reprojection is not exact and requires bilinear filtering for reconstruction, each reprojection step introduces a slight blur [YNS*09]. Furthermore, the influence of the new samples becomes close to zero, and old samples never get replaced. Therefore we clamp n_t to a user-defined threshold n_{max}, which causes the influence of older contributions to decay over time. Thus, $conv(p) = min(n_t(p), n_{max})/n_{max}$ is an indicator of the state of convergence. Note that, for $n_{max} \to \infty$ Equation 5.7 would converge to the correct solution - unlike the exponential smoothing used in previous approaches [SJW07, NSL*07], which acts as a temporal filter kernel.

In our experience, a threshold n_{max} in the range [500..1500] provides a sufficiently fast update frequency to avoid major blurring artifacts while avoiding undersampling artifacts like temporal flickering. Figure 5.4 (left)

Chapter 5. High Quality Screen-Space Ambient Occlusion using Temporal Coherence

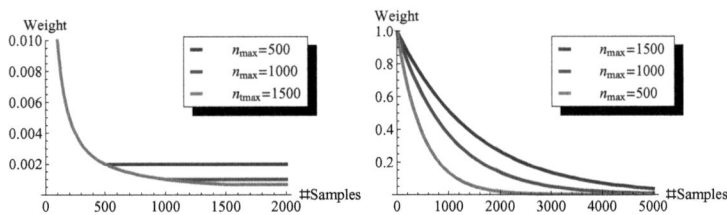

Figure 5.4: The weight ($1/n_t$) of a new sample (top) and of an old AO solution (bottom) after given number of samples using thresholds $n_{max} = 500, 1000, 1500$.

depicts how the influence of a new sample changes from the moment it is introduced, and (right) the exponential decay of the influence of the old AO solution after the threshold n_{max} was reached.

5.2.4 Detecting and dealing with invalid pixels

When reprojecting a fragment, we need to check whether the cached AO value is valid. If it is not, n_t is reset to 0 and a new AO solution is computed. We need to check two conditions: disocclusions and changes in the sample neighborhood.

5.2.4.1 Detecting disocclusions

Previous approaches [SJW07, NSL*07] check for disocclusions by comparing the depth of the reprojected fragment position d to the depth of the cached value d_{prev}:

$$|d - d_{prev}| < \epsilon$$

However, we found that neither screen-space depth values nor eye-linear depth values gave reliable results. Screen-space depth values are only accurate in a small region around the near plane, while eye-linear depth comparisons are overly sensitive in regions near the far plane and not sensitive enough near the near plane. The solution is to store eye-linear depth val-

5.2. Our algorithm

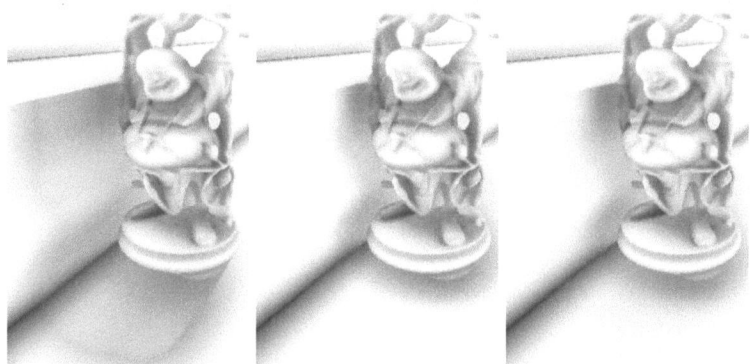

Figure 5.5: If we do not check for disocclusions due to dynamic objects in the area surrounding the current pixel, we get strong artifacts (left). A full invalidation removes the artifacts, but the shadow regions cannot profit much from temporal coherence (middle). Assigning a small weight to the invalidated pixels allows for a smooth invalidation and solves both problems (right).

ues, but to consider *relative* depth differences instead of absolute ones, by checking for

$$|1 - \frac{d}{d_{prev}}| < \epsilon, \tag{5.8}$$

which gives good results even for large scenes with a wide depth range. Note that pixels which were outside the frame buffer in the previous frame are also marked as invalid.

5.2.4.2 Detecting Changes in the Neighborhood

Testing for disocclusion is a sufficient condition for validity in a purely static scene, or for pure antialiasing. However, for shading kernels that access neighboring pixels in dynamic scenes, like SSAO, we have to take into account that the shading of the current pixel can be affected by nearby moving objects, even if there is no disocclusion. Consider for example a scene where

Chapter 5. High Quality Screen-Space Ambient Occlusion using Temporal Coherence

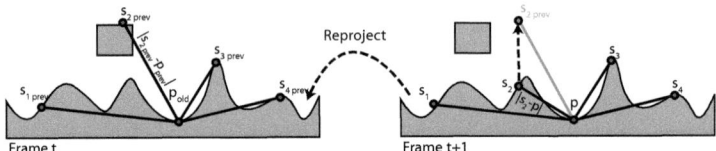

Figure 5.6: The distance of p to sample point s_2 in the current frame differs significantly from the previous frame, hence we assume that a local change of geometry occurred, which affects the shading of p.

a box is lifted from the floor. The SSAO values of pixels in the contact shadow area surrounding the box change even if there is no disocclusion of the pixel itself. The artifacts that result from ignoring this problem can be seen in Figure 5.5, left. The rendering quality can be further improved by using smooth invalidation (defined in Section 5.2.6), as can be seen in the rightmost image of Figure 5.5.

The size of the neighborhood to check is equivalent to the size of the sampling kernel used for SSAO. Checking the complete neighborhood of a pixel would be prohibitively expensive, therefore we use sampling. Actually, it turns out that we already have a set of samples, namely the ones used for AO generation. That means that we effectively use our AO sampling kernel for two purposes: for computing the current contribution $C_t(p)$, and to test for validity. A pixel p is considered to be valid for a sample s_i if the relative positions of sample and pixel have not changed by more than ϵ (see Figure 5.6):

$$||s_i - p| - |s_{iprev} - p_{prev}|| < \epsilon, \qquad (5.9)$$

where the reprojected position s_{iprev} is computed from the offset vector stored for s_i (recall that the first rendering pass stores the offset vectors for all pixels in the frame buffer for later access by the SSAO shading pass). Note that we therefore use only those samples for the neighborhood test that lie in front of the tangent plane of p, since only those samples actually modify the shadow term. If this test fails for one of the samples evaluated for pixel

5.2. Our algorithm

Figure 5.7: This figure shows pixels recently invalidated by our algorithm. The left image depicts a rotation, the middle image a translation, and the right image an animated (walking) character. Red pixels were invalidated more recently than black ones while white pixels are sufficiently converged.

p, then p is marked invalid and n_t is set to 0.

Note that, in order to avoid one costly texture look up when fetching p_{prev}, the required values for this test and for the ambient occlusion computation should be stored in a single render target.

In the case of dynamic objects, a large portion of the pixel information from the previous frame is typically reusable. See Figure 5.7 for a visualization of recently invalidated regions. E.g., for rotational movements, disocclusions occur on the silhouette, or at pixels that were hidden by creases or folds on the surface in previous frames. The amount of disocclusion depends on the speed of rotation, and is usually reasonably low for up to some degrees per frame. Theoretically we could also check if the angle between surface normal and vector to sample has changed by a significant amount from one frame to the next to detect more cases. However, that would require more information to be stored (surface normal of old pixel), and in all our tests we found it sufficient to test for condition 5.9.

5.2.5 Dealing with undersampled regions

Our algorithm ensures high-quality AO for sufficiently converged pixels. However, in screen regions that have been invalidated recently, the undersampling may result in temporal flickering. Disoccluded regions are often coherent and lead to distracting correlated noise patterns over several frames. We solve

Chapter 5. High Quality Screen-Space Ambient Occlusion using Temporal Coherence

this by a new convergence-aware spatial filter and by adaptive sampling.

5.2.5.1 Adaptive Convergence-Aware Spatial Filter

SSAO methods usually apply a spatial filtering pass after shading computations in order to prevent noise artifacts caused by insufficient sampling rates. We also apply spatial filtering, but only as long as the temporal coherence is not sufficient. Frequently used choices of filters are variants of the cross bilateral filter [ED04, BSD08], where filtering over edges is avoided by taking the depth differences into account. Although this filter is not formally separable, in a real-time setting it is usually applied separately in x and y directions to make evaluation feasible. We follow this approach, too.

In contrast to previous approaches, we have additional information for the filter which can greatly reduce noise: the *convergence conv(p)* of our AO values. Recently disoccluded pixels (e.g., in a thin silhouette region) can gather more information from nearby converged pixels instead of from other unreliable pixels. Furthermore, we apply the filter kernel directly to world-space distances, which automatically takes depth differences into account:

$$AO_{filt}(p) = \frac{1}{k(x,p)} \sum_{x \in F} g(|p-x|) conv(x) AO(x), \quad (5.10)$$

where x are the individual filter samples in the screen-space support F of the filter (e.g., a 9x9 pixel region), $k(x,p)$ is the normalization $\sum_{x \in F} g(|p-x|) conv(x)$, and g is a spatial filter kernel (e.g., a Gaussian). As a pixel gets more converged, we shrink the screen-space filter support smoothly using the shrinking factor s:

$$s(p) = \frac{\max(c_{adaptive} - conv(p), 0)}{c_{adaptive}}, \quad (5.11)$$

so that when convergence has reached $c_{adaptive}$, we turn off spatial filtering completely. We found the setting of $c_{adaptive}$ to be perceptually uncritical, e.g., 0.2 leads to unnoticeable transitions.

5.2. Our algorithm

parameter name	value
Initial samples k_1	32
Converged samples k_2	8–16
Threshold $c_{adaptive}$	0.2
Threshold $c_{spatial}$	0.3
Threshold c_{rot}	0.5
n_{max}	500–1500
Filter width F	$9x9$

Table 5.1: Recommended parameters for our method.

5.2.5.2 Adaptive Sampling

While spatial filtering can reduce noise, it is even better to provide more input samples. We adapt the number k of new AO samples per frame depending on convergence (note that these samples are completely unrelated to the screen-space samples used for spatial filtering in the previous section, where the kernel size is adapted instead of changing the number of samples). Since disoccluded regions are often spatially coherent (as can be seen in Figure 5.7), the required dynamic branching operations in the shader are efficient on today's graphics hardware.

Note that it is necessary to generate at least a minimum amount of samples for the same reasons that we clamp $n_t(p)$ in Equation 5.6, i.e., to avoid blurring artifacts introduced by bilinear filtering. Furthermore, a certain number of samples is required for detecting invalid pixels due to changing neighborhoods (Section 5.2.4.2). In order to keep branching to a minimum, we chose a simple two-stage scheme, with k_1 samples if $conv(p) < c_{spatial}$ and k_2 samples otherwise (refer to Table 5.1 for a list of parameters actually used in our implementation).

5.2.6 Optimizations

In this section we describe some optimizations that allow for faster frame rates or better image quality. As in most AO approaches, we rotate the sampling pattern by a different random vector for each input pixel. However, this leads to a surprisingly large performance hit, supposedly due to texture

Chapter 5. High Quality Screen-Space Ambient Occlusion using Temporal Coherence

cache thrashing [SW09]. Therefore we turn off the rotation once convergence reaches a certain threshold c_{rot}.

For moderately fast moving objects, the ambient occlusion is perceptually valid for more than one frame. If only the neighborhood changes (i.e., the second condition for invalidation from Section 5.2.4), a full invalidation of the current pixel is a waste of useful information, and flickering artifacts may occur. Instead of fully discarding the current solution by resetting n_t to 0, we rather clamp n_t to a low value (between 32 and 64). Note that in practice, we do not clamp but reduce n_{max} for a single frame. Using this small optimization, the AO will appear smoother over time. Hence we denote it as *smooth invalidation*. The resulting slight motion blur effect is much less distracting than temporal flickering. We found a value in the range of n_{max} between 32 and 64 to be a good tradeoff between the two extrema (see Figure 5.5, right). A weak invalidation is especially helpful for animated sequences where the transitions stay smooth.

A problem inherent in SSAO is the handling of samples that extend beyond the frame buffer borders. As there is no best method, we settle for reusing the values that appeared on the border by using clamp-to-edge. To avoid artifacts on the edges of the screen due to the missing depth information, we can optionally compute a slightly larger image than we finally display on the screen – it is sufficient to extend about 5–10% on each side of the screen depending on the size of the SSAO kernel and the near plane. Note that this is a general problem of SSAO and not a restriction caused by our algorithm. Because these border samples carry incorrect information that should not be propagated, we detect those samples that were outside the frame buffer in the previous frame using our invalidation scheme (see Section 5.2.4).

5.3 Results

We implemented the proposed method in OpenGL using the Cg shading language, and tested it on two scenes of different characteristics (shown in Figure 5.8), the Sibenik cathedral and the Vienna city model. Both scenes

5.3. Results

Figure 5.8: Used test scenes: Sibenik cathedral (7,013,932 vertices) and Vienna (21,934,980 vertices).

were populated with several dynamic objects. For all our tests we used an Intel Core 2 processor at 2.66 GHz (using 1 core) and an NVIDIA GeForce 280 GTX graphics board. The resolution of our render targets is either 1024x768 or 800x600, and we used 32 bit precision for all our render targets. We also implemented a version that computes SSAO on a half resolution render target and upsamples the solution for the final image using our spatial filter.

To prove that our method is mostly independent of the SSAO generation method, we implemented both the method of Ritschel et al.[RGS09], and the algorithm introduced by Fox and Compton [FC08]. The latter algorithm uses screen-space sampling like Shanmugam and Arikan [SA07], and is more of an artistic approach and less physically based. In our opinion it preserves more small details when using large kernels for capturing low-frequency AO. In order to ensure that the sampling kernel will always cover the same size in world space, we implemented the following extension to the method: we multiply the initial kernel radius with the w coordinate from the perspective projection of the current pixel, i.e., the perspective foreshortening factor. As a result we obtain AO values that are invariant to zooming.

Our method has a couple of parameters used to control temporal refinement, which we list in Table 5.1 together with some recommended values.

In the two walkthrough sequences for Vienna and Sibenik, we aimed to consider all the major cases of motion that occur in real-world applications.

Chapter 5. High Quality Screen-Space Ambient Occlusion using Temporal Coherence

Scene	Sibenik (7,013,932 vertices)		
resolution	SSAO	TSSAO	Deferred
1024 x 768	23 FPS	36 FPS	62 FPS
800 x 600	35 FPS	60 FPS	90 FPS
800 x 600 halfres	64 FPS	74 FPS	
Scene	Vienna (21,934,980 vertices)		
resolution	SSAO	TSSAO	Deferred
1024 x 768	21 FPS	25 FPS	65 FPS
800 x 600	29 FPS	34 FPS	67 FPS
800 x 600 halfres	47 FPS	49 FPS	

Table 5.2: Average timings for the two used walkthrough sequences. We compare standard SSAO, our method (TSSAO), and deferred shading without SSAO as a baseline. For SSAO we used 32 samples in all scenes. For TSSAO we used 8–32 samples for TSSAO in the Vienna scene and 16–32 samples in the Sibenik cathedral.

We included rigid dynamic objects as well as animated characters with deforming parts.

Table 5.2 shows average timings of our walkthroughs, comparing our method (TSSAO) with SSAO without temporal coherence and the performance-baseline method: deferred shading without SSAO. TSSAO used 8 respectively 16 samples when converged and 32 otherwise for Vienna and for Sibenik, whereas SSAO always uses 32 samples. The cost of the SSAO/TSSAO algorithms (difference in frame times to baseline) is relatively independent of the scene complexity, and scales with the number of pixels in the frame buffer. TSSAO is always faster than SSAO when using the same number of samples, for full and for half resolution ambient occlusion buffers. TSSAO does not apply spatial filtering or rotate the sampling filter kernel after convergence has been reached.

Figure 5.9 shows the frame time variations for both walkthroughs. Note that occlusion culling is enabled for the large-scale Vienna model, and thus the frame rate for the baseline deferred shading is quite high for such a complex model. The framerate variations for TSSAO stem from the fact that the method generates adaptively more samples for recently disoccluded regions, which can be quite big if we have dynamic objects that are large in

5.3. Results

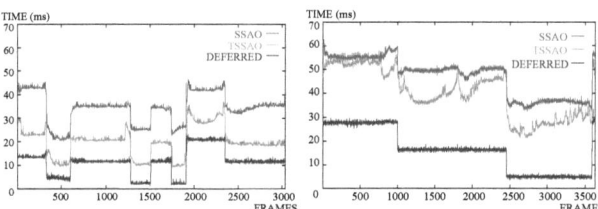

Figure 5.9: Frame times of the Vienna walkthrough (with occlusion culling, left) and the Sibenik walkthrough (right) at resolution 1024x768.

Figure 5.10: Rotational movement using TSSAO. (left) Without filter. (right) Using our filter. Note how the filter is only applied in the noisy regions, while the rest stays crisp (Zoom into the pdf to see the differences).

screen space. For close-ups of dynamic objects, the frame times of TSSAO are almost as long as the frame times of SSAO. For more static parts of the scenes, TSSAO is significantly faster.

Figure 5.10 depicts the influence of the adaptive convergence-aware filter on the quality of the TSSAO solution.

The quality of TSSAO is significantly better. It corresponds to at least a 32 sample SSAO solution (since 32 samples are used for disocclusions), while the converged state takes up to several hundred (n_{max}) samples into account. Note that a similar quality SSAO solution would be prohibitively slow. As can be seen in Figure 5.1 (using the method of Fox and Compton)

169

Chapter 5. High Quality Screen-Space Ambient Occlusion using Temporal Coherence

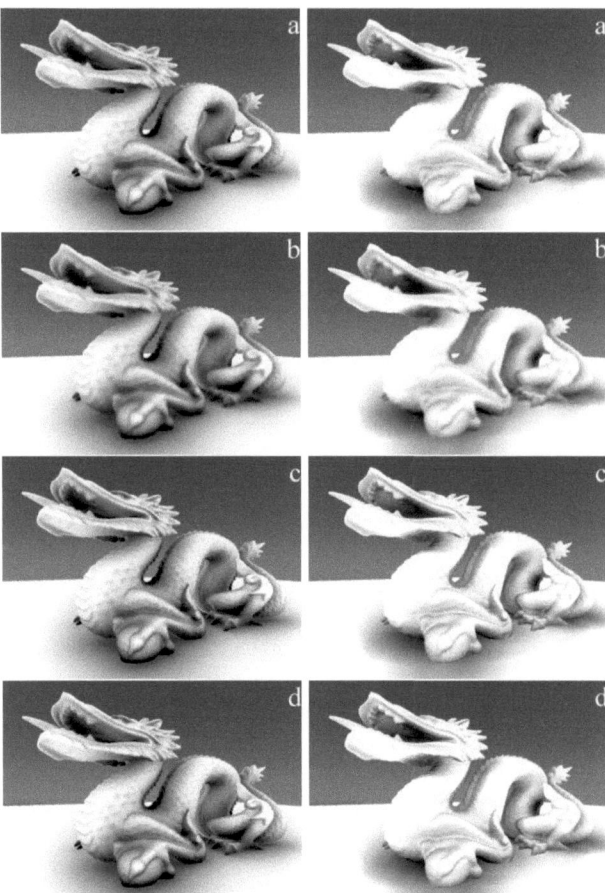

Figure 5.11: From left to right: SSAO without temporal coherence using 32 samples, with a (a) weak, (b) strong blur. (c) TSSAO using 8 - 32 samples per frame. (d) Reference solution using 480 samples. The results are shown for the methods of Fox and Compton (left column) and Ritschel et al. (right column). All at 1024x768 resolution.

and Figure 5.11 (using either the method of Fox and Compton or the method of Ritschel et al.), TSSAO provides finer details and less noise artifacts, while at the same time being faster. We compared TSSAO to SSAO with a weak and a strong blur filter, and to a reference solution using 480 samples per frame – which was the highest number of samples our shader could compute. After a short time, the TSSAO method converges to the reference solution.

5.4 Conclusion

We presented a screen-space ambient occlusion algorithm that utilizes reprojection and temporal coherence to produce high-quality ambient occlusion for dynamic scenes. Our algorithm reuses available sample information from previous frames if available, while adaptively generating more samples and applying spatial filtering only in the regions where not enough samples have been accumulated yet. We have shown an efficient new pixel validity test for shading algorithms, which accesses a pixel neighborhood in a way that it can also benefit from temporal reprojection. While we restricted our results to show ambient occlusion, our algorithm can be seen as a cookbook recipe that is applicable to many other screen-space sampling algorithms with a finite kernel size.

In the future, we want to explore other useful sampling-based techniques and how they can be enhanced with temporal coherence, and aim to derive general rules regarding invalidation that are applicable to different classes of problems. Also we plan to further investigate the problems with the blurriness that occurs because of bilinear filtering in combination with fast zooms. As these artifacts mainly occur on surfaces that are nearly perpendicular to the view direction, we want to investigate how they are related to the *projection error* known from shadow mapping.

Chapter 5. High Quality Screen-Space Ambient Occlusion using Temporal Coherence

*You're invisible now,
you got no secrets to conceal.*

Bob Dylan

6

Conclusions and Future Work

In the final chapter we first sum up the contents of the thesis. Then we give a detailed analysis of the strengths and limitations of the proposed algorithms and show future directions. Finally we give some conclusions.

6.1 Synopsis

In this thesis we discussed visibility computations in their various forms of occurrence, both qualitative and quantitative in nature, and why this task is so fundamental for the field of realistic 3D computer graphics. The main part of our research was focussed on the task of qualitative visibility, i.e., visibility culling for rendering acceleration, both as a preprocess and online. As countless algorithms have been already published in the field of visibility preprocessing, we pointed out the comparable importance of the task of *preparing* the scene for the actual PVS computation by creating meaningful view cells and objects. Another part of this thesis dealt with online occlusion culling methods for fully dynamic scenes, and how to reduce the overhead of hardware occlusion queries to make them compatible to preprocessed visibility in terms of ease of use and efficiency. Also, we investigated quantitative visibility computations for realistic lighting effects and ambient occlusion in particular, as this is nothing else than pure visibility over the hemisphere. Temporal coherence was a recurring term in this thesis - we used its potential to accelerate both online occlusion culling and screen-space ambient

Chapter 6. Conclusions and Future Work

occlusion, while significantly improving the quality of the latter technique.

Our goal was to create general and practical algorithms for *output sensitive* real-time rendering that have no restrictions with respect to the scene configuration. In particular, we proposed four novel visibility algorithms which cover a wide range of applications. We will now shortly summarize them, and describe their main contributions.

Two algorithms deal with the creation of view space and objects space partitions that are optimal for subsequent PVS-based rendering in terms of render cost and memory cost. To our knowledge these are the first methods which analyze what good view and object space partitions are in terms of render cost and memory cost, and then optimize these partitions for visibility culling. Both algorithms start with an initial coarse global visibility sampling in order to capture sufficient information about the visibility in the scene. A novel cost-benefit model is then used to drive the partitioning process. The first method assumes the objects to be given and provides a visibility guided view cell construction. First it subdivides the scene into a set of elementary view cells using a BSP tree, and then optionally merges these cells to larger ones for further refinement. We extended this method to allow for *combined optimization* of view space and object space, by interleaving the subdivision process. This is the first algorithm that accounts for the fact that render cost and memory cost in a scene are highly dependent on the interaction of *both* subdivisions. Next we presented a fast online culling algorithm that improves the well-known Coherent Hierarchical Culling (CHC) algorithm, which utilizes temporal coherence by waiting only for the query results of the previously invisible nodes, and interleaves querying and rendering. The new algorithm, CHC++, keeps the general structure of the original algorithm and its simplicity, while eliminating most of its drawbacks by introducing a couple of optimizations. The main contribution is a significant reduction of the algorithm overhead even for difficult view points compared to previous approaches. At last we presented a screen-space ambient occlusion algorithm that employs temporal reprojection to exploit coherence between consecutive frames and accumulates samples over time. We introduced a novel invalidation scheme which allows for fully dynamic scenes and deformable objects.

Furthermore, we introduced an adaptive spatial filter as well as an adaptive sampling strategy to generally raise the quality of any underlying SSAO shading technique while regenerating only the minimal amount of samples.

6.2 Analysis of the proposed algorithms

The methods for scene preprocessing provide valuable insight into the properties of view space and object space, their dual relationship, and how they are connected in terms of render cost and memory consumption. We defined a measure for optimality of view space and object space partitions, and showed that traditional methods for view space subdivision like autopartition BSP are far from optimal under these assumptions. While grid-like structures work quite well in outdoor scenes with a lot of free space, aligning the locations of the view cell boundaries with actual visibility events is more important in scenarios with sudden changes in visibility like indoor scenes. We believe that our algorithms are well suited to be used in a frame work in combination with the efficient AGVS visibility solver [BMW*09], as both methods use similar strategies, i.e., random global sampling and hierarchical subdivision. While we achieved some decent results with our techniques, we feel that there is future work to do in order to make good estimates of render cost, and to calibrate the heuristics for a particular hardware, taking material properties and LODs into account. The method for view cell construction may have more practical relevance than the second method that interleaves view space and object space subdivisions, because such a combined optimization of view space and objects space is computationally much more expensive.

We believe that CHC++, our online occlusion culling algorithm, is efficient and useful in practice. It was developed in the context of practical issues that we faced when integrating CHC into a game engine. Hence we are quite confident that it can be implemented into any game engine with moderate effort and without major modifications. The main observation of the work was to realize that much of the query overhead is caused by the state changes induced by switches between render and query mode. Hence

Chapter 6. Conclusions and Future Work

Figure 6.1: As can be seen in this snapshot, our real-time-rendering frame work features techniques like shadow mapping and SSAO for realistic lighting (i.e., quantitative visibility). The core rendering algorithm uses visibility culling for acceleration (i.e., qualitative visibility).

the most effective optimization is the batching of occlusion queries, which significantly reduces the number of these costly state changes compared to the previous state of the art. The algorithms limits the overhead of the occlusion queries to a minimum, and achieves a significant speed up over algorithms like CHC or NOHC on various target hardwares.

Our temporal screen-space ambient occlusion (TSSAO) algorithm is also well suited for use in practice. The method greatly enhances the quality of the underlying SSAO algorithm [FC08, RGS09] due to the fact that hundreds of samples can be accumulated over a couple of frames. In fact, a similar technique was developed in parallel for use in the high-profile game Star Craft 2 [SW09], which underlines the relevance of our method. Thanks to our novel invalidation scheme, our method works can handle dynamic scenes and deformable objects very well. As a screen-space algorithm, it is more or less independent of the scene size, and can be used together with CHC++ to render large dynamic scenes with realistic lighting in an output-sensitive fashion and in real-time frame rates.

6.2.1 Combining our algorithms

As each of our proposed algorithms covers a different aspect of visibility computations, it is quite straightforward to combine them and to provide a system for output-sensitive real-time rendering with advanced shading techniques. In fact, we have developed a rendering framework that supports both PVS-based rendering for the static geometry and online culling using CHC++, and they can optionally be used together. The framework has a deferred rendering pipeline that utilizes shadow mapping for direct lighting, and our screen-space ambient occlusion algorithm for the indirect illumination. Our visibility culling algorithms (i.e., qualitative visibility) work very well together with our real-time illumination algorithms (i.e., quantitative visibility), because all these algorithms are output-sensitive and more or less independent of the scene size (as long as the scene fits into memory). A rendering using our frame work can be seen in Figure 6.1.

To integrate the PVSs into our framework we established a pipeline that first computes the view cells for a given scene using our view cell construction algorithm. Then it feeds these optimized view cells to the visibility solver (i.e., the efficient AGVS algorithm [BMW*09]), which computes a good solution in less than two hours. At last it loads the solution (consisting of the view cells and the corresponding PVSs) into our online rendering framework, where the task is just to find the current view cell and load its PVS.

We combine PVS-based rendering with CHC++ by setting a flag which indicates for each object in the scene if it is potentially visible. Then we simply proceed with the hierarchical traversal of CHC++, and process only objects that are potentially visible. For difficult view points combining preprocessing and CHC++ brings some gain compared to CHC++ alone, whereas there is practically no gain for situations where online occlusion culling works best (e.g., in the streets of a city). However, once we integrate pre-fetching into our framework for memory-intensive scenes, we expect that PVSs will be very useful for the purpose of prediction.

6.3 Future work

This section discusses the future outlooks on visibility research. Although many believe that this topic has already reached a rather mature state, we identified several issues that ought to be solved in order to make visibility

Chapter 6. Conclusions and Future Work

culling more feasible in practical applications. Afterwards, we give an outlook on other topics that have been discussed in this thesis, in particular real-time global illumination and reprojection techniques.

6.3.1 Striving for simplicity

A very important criterion for the success of a technique is its *simplicity* and *ease of use*. Occam's razor states that the simplest solutions are often the best, and historically it has been shown that the simplest algorithms are those that survive in time, whereas more sophisticated algorithms rarely come to any practical use (e.g., the z-buffer [Cat75] versus the a-buffer [Car84]). While some efficient visibility algorithms have been proposed, they are often still hard to implement and difficult to debug, which to some extend limits their widespread use. A first step into the right direction was made in recent years when favoring conceptionally simpler sampling-based visibility algorithms over geometric algorithms that often instable and require special handling for occluder fusion. Also, visibility algorithms should get rid of special structures like hierarchies, stacks, or caches wherever possible. This will improve their chances to scale better with very complex scenes and new hardware developments like massively parallel hardware algorithms.

6.3.2 A combined algorithm using PVSs and hardware occlusion queries

Just using PVS-based rendering together with CHC++ without any modifications brings only a minimal speedup in most situations, and there seems to be quite limited potential to improve on previous online culling algorithms with means of temporal coherence only. However, it may be possible to combine online culling and visibility preprocessing in a more radical way in a single algorithm, which retains the strength of both paradigms while getting rid of the weaknesses. Combining a method similar to CHC++ with a view cell structure and a coarse form of PVSs (i.e., making use of spatial coherence) could be the way to go, yielding some speedup over CHC++, while

6.3. Future work

avoiding the rare situations that the overhead of CHC++ may still dominate the gain, like in extreme bird eye views of city scenes. Such an algorithm could also be made simpler than current preprocessing and online occlusion culling methods, hence fulfilling the requirements of the last paragraph.

6.3.3 Reverse visibility for interactive scene editing

An interesting topic yet not fully explored by the research community is the *reversal* of the visibility problem, i.e., to *design* the visibility in a scene in order to fit the needs of a user. This task has an important application in game design, where the designers want to avoid annoying frame rate drops [ED07] due to portions of the scene that are unintentionally visible through leaks. The problem was partly handled by recent visibility algorithms [ED07, BMW*09]. The latter method is able to interactively visualize so-called *visibility hotspots* (i.e., regions where the PVSs are too large) in the scene, and locally recalculate visibility in the regions of changes. However, the focus of this work was PVS computation, and the ability for interactive visibility-aware scene manipulation is still in a rather rudimentary state. Much more work and research must still be put into a complete system that will be useful in the work flow of a game company. Ideally, there could be a plug-in for a major rendering package that allows for visibility-aware scene editing.

6.3.4 Optimal hierarchy construction for online culling

Online culling algorithms have already reached a very advanced state, and we feel that more potential lies in optimizing the underlying hierarchy than in optimizing the actual algorithm. Up to now there is only a very small number of papers available on this topic, most notably the survey of Meißner et al. [MBM*01]. However, they did not take hardware-dependent parameters into account for their heuristics. The properties of the hierarchy, like the proper termination depth, can significantly influence the performance of an occlusion culling algorithm. The optimal parameters depend on the occlusion

Chapter 6. Conclusions and Future Work

properties in the scene, the cost of a query, the cost of rendering and shading the geometry. An important question is how to best handle materials.

6.3.5 Robust and efficient exact visibility

While exact visibility has already been claimed to be solved, we are not aware of any solution that can handle general 3D scenes with millions of triangles. Also, these algorithms are prone to numerical instabilities. It is still not known if an efficient exact solution that scales well with scene size, has little or no numerical problems, and reasonable memory requirements, is even possible. Without doubt such an algorithm would solve a number of issues in the field of visibility. For example, statistics over the PVS size lose some significance if there is no comparison to a ground truth solution, because the exact PVS size is not known or unreliable. Therefore we believe that it may be worthwhile to examine exact algorithms further. Hopefully new parallel programming interfaces like CUDA or new architectures like NVidia Tesla and ATI FireStream open up new possibilities in this direction.

6.3.6 Real-time global illumination

Recent developments make it a viable option in the future to routinely use dynamic real-time global illumination in standard applications and consumer games. It is already possible to evaluate hundreds of visibility queries per frame in almost real time using imperfect shadow maps [RGS09]. Hence it seems that the techniques are already there, and it is just a question of more powerful hardware to reach this goal. On a closer look however, it becomes apparent that current real-time solutions are merely a crude approximation of full-fledged global illumination, and that there is still a sufficient amount of tough problems for researchers to solve in this field. A trend is visible in recent years that goes into the direction of investigating algorithms and effects that exist since a long time in offline rendering, and mapping them to real-time algorithms on modern hardware architectures, using APIs like CUDA.

6.3.7 Reprojection and temporal coherence

Of course there are limits to the extent to which we can exploit temporal coherence to reuse results from previous frames - but we have yet to find out where these limits lie. It seems that the properties of reprojection techniques are not fully understood yet, and a more detailed analysis can bring more insights, and hopefully allows a more robust and better use of this powerful class of methods. In particular, one has to investigate the influence of the projection error due to steep surfaces on the approximation error, resulting in blur artifacts. The same is true for the influence of all kinds of motions of both viewer and objects.

6.4 Conclusions

This thesis presented many aspects of visibility computations for real-time rendering. We showed that virtually all areas of 3D computer graphics require solving complex visibility interactions efficiently and in an intelligent fashion, and we proposed solutions for several important visibility problems. New applications require processing huge amounts of data interactively and pose challenges to both current and future visibility research. It is important to see that ray tracing is not the holy grail when it comes to visualizing large data sets. Using hierarchical visibility culling together with a simplification strategy like LODs for distant objects, rasterization-based rendering scales equally well, and is able to render large scenes with hundreds of millions of triangles at real-time frame rates. The first part of this thesis was dedicated to the problem of visibility culling for output-sensitive rendering. We showed that both big paradigms of visibility culling, preprocessing and online occlusion culling, have important applications and interesting research problems, and presented contributions in both areas that take general 3D scenes as input. The second part of the thesis investigated visibility computations for the purpose of realistic lighting. The proposed ambient occlusion algorithm showed that by utilizing temporal coherence, accurate high-quality shading with effectively hundreds of queries per pixel is possible at real-time frame

Chapter 6. Conclusions and Future Work

rates. As a screen-space method, the presented algorithm is naturally output sensitive and more or less independent of scene size. Hence all our methods thrive for output sensitivity and can be combined for maximal efficiency, using preprocessing for the static parts of the scene, online culling for the dynamic parts, and ambient occlusion for realistic lighting. On the one hand, this thesis provided some practical solutions for typical visibility problems that accelerate rendering and improve the rendering quality. On the other hand, it contributed some theoretical aspects and brings deeper understanding of the properties of visibility culling, and will hopefully inspire researchers to continue visibility research into new fruitful directions in the future.

Bibliography

[AAT93] ABRAMS S., ALLEN P., TARABANIS K.: Dynamic sensor planning. In *DARPA93* (1993), pp. 599–607.

[Abr96] ABRASH M.: Inside quake: Visible surface determination. In *Dr. Dobb's Sourcebook January/February 1996* (1996), pp. 41–45.

[Ail00] AILA T.: *SurRender Umbra: A Visibility Determination Framework for Dynamic Environments*. Master's thesis, Helsinki University of Technology, 2000.

[AM00] ASSARSSON U., MÖLLER T.: Optimized view frustum culling algorithms for bounding boxes. *Journal of graphics, gpu, and game tools 5*, 1 (2000), 9–22.

[AM04] AILA T., MIETTINEN V.: dpvs: An occlusion culling system for massive dynamic environments. *IEEE Comput. Graph. Appl. 24*, 2 (2004), 86–97.

[AMB*07] ANNEN T., MERTENS T., BEKAERT P., SEIDEL H.-P., KAUTZ J.: Convolution shadow maps. In *Rendering Techniques 2007: Eurographics Symposium on Rendering* (Grenoble, France, June 2007), Kautz J., Pattanaik S., (Eds.), vol. 18 of *Eurographics / ACM SIGGRAPH Symposium Proceedings*, Eurographics, pp. 51–60.

[ARB90] AIREY J. M., ROHLF J. H., BROOKS, JR. F. P.: Towards image realism with interactive update rates in complex virtual building environments. In *1990 Symposium on Interactive 3D Graphics* (1990), ACM SIGGRAPH, pp. 41–50. Also available as Technical Report TR-90-001, Computer Science Department, University of North Carolina.

[ATS94] ARVO J., TORRANCE K., SMITS B.: A framework for the analysis of error in global illumination algorithms. In *SIGGRAPH '94: Proceedings of the 21st annual conference on Computer graphics and interactive techniques* (New York, NY, USA, 1994), ACM, pp. 75–84.

[BCS08] BAVOIL L., CALLAHAN S. P., SILVA C. T.: Robust soft shadow mapping with backprojection and depth peeling. *journal of graphics, gpu, and game tools 13*, 1 (2008), 19–30.

[BFMZ94] BISHOP G., FUCHS H., MCMILLAN L., ZAGIER E. J. S.: Frameless rendering: double buffering considered harmful. In *SIGGRAPH '94: Proceedings of the 21st annual conference on Computer graphics and interactive techniques* (New York, NY, USA, 1994), ACM, pp. 175–176.

Bibliography

[BHP07] BRÜDERLIN B., HEYER M., PFÜTZNER S.: Interviews3d: A platform for interactive handling of massive data sets. *IEEE Comput. Graph. Appl. 27*, 6 (2007), 48–59.

[Bit03] BITTNER J.: *Hierarchical Techniques for Visibility Computations*. PhD thesis, Czech Technical University in Prague, 2003.

[BMH98] BARTZ D., MEISSNER M., HÜTTNER T.: Extending graphics hardware for occlusion queries in opengl. In *HWWS '98: Proceedings of the ACM SIGGRAPH/EUROGRAPHICS workshop on Graphics hardware* (New York, NY, USA, 1998), ACM Press, pp. 97–ff.

[BMW*09] BITTNER J., MATTAUSCH O., WONKA P., HAVRAN V., WIMMER M.: Adaptive global visibility sampling. In *SIGGRAPH '09: ACM SIGGRAPH 2009 Papers* (New York, NY, USA, 2009), ACM.

[BSD08] BAVOIL L., SAINZ M., DIMITROV R.: Image-space horizon-based ambient occlusion. In *SIGGRAPH '08: ACM SIGGRAPH 2008 talks* (New York, NY, USA, 2008), ACM, pp. 1–1.

[BSGM02] BAXTER W., SUD A., GOVINDARAJU N., MANOCHA D.: Gigawalk: Interactive walkthrough of complex environments, 2002.

[Bun05] BUNNELL M.: *Dynamic Ambient Occlusion and Indirect Lighting*. Addison-Wesley Professional, 2005, ch. 14, pp. 223–233.

[BW03] BITTNER J., WONKA P.: Visibility in computer graphics. *Environment and Planning B: Planning and Design 30*, 5 (sep 2003), 729–756.

[BWPP04] BITTNER J., WIMMER M., PIRINGER H., PURGATHOFER W.: Coherent hierarchical culling: Hardware occlusion queries made useful. *Computer Graphics Forum 23*, 3 (Sept. 2004), 615–624. Proceedings EUROGRAPHICS 2004.

[BWW01] BITTNER J., WONKA P., WIMMER M.: Visibility preprocessing for urban scenes using line space subdivision. In *Proceedings of Pacific Graphics (PG'01)* (Tokyo, Japan, 2001), IEEE Computer Society, pp. 276–284.

[BWW05] BITTNER J., WONKA P., WIMMER M.: Fast exact from-region visibility in urban scenes. In *Rendering Techniques 2005 (Proceedings Eurographics Symposium on Rendering)* (June 2005), Bala K., Dutré P., (Eds.), Eurographics, Eurographics Association, pp. 223–230.

[CAB00] CARLOS ANDÚJAR CARLOS SAONA-VÁZQUEZ I. N., BRUNET P.: Integrating occlusion culling with levels of detail through hardly-visible sets. In *Computer Graphics Forum (Proceedings of Eurographics 2000)* (2000), pp. 499–506.

Bibliography

[Car84] CARPENTER L.: The A-buffer, an antialiased hidden surface method. In *Computer Graphics (SIGGRAPH '84 Proceedings)* (July 1984), Christiansen H., (Ed.), vol. 18, pp. 103–108.

[Cat75] CATMULL E. E.: Computer display of curved surfaces. In *Proceedings of the IEEE Conference on Computer Graphics, Pattern Recognition, and Data Structure* (May 1975), pp. 11–17.

[CATM09] CHANDAK A., ANTANI L., TAYLOR M., MANOCHA D.: Fastv: From-point visibility culling on complex models. *Computer Graphics Forum (Proceedings EGSR 2009) 27*, 4 (June 2009).

[CBWR07] CHARALAMBOS J. P., BITTNER J., WIMMER M., ROMERO E.: Optimized hlod refinement driven by hardware occlusion queries. In *Symposium on Visual Computing, (to appear)* (2007).

[CDP95] CAZALS F., DRETTAKIS G., PUECH C.: Filtering, clustering and hierarchy construction: a new solution for ray-tracing complex scenes. *Computer Graphics Forum 14*, 3 (1995), 371–382.

[COCSD02] COHEN-OR D., CHRYSANTHOU Y., SILVA C., DURAND F.: A survey of visibility for walkthrough applications. *IEEE Transactions on Visualization and Computer Graphics.* (2002).

[COFHZ98] COHEN-OR D., FIBICH G., HALPERIN D., ZADICARIO E.: Conservative visibility and strong occlusion for viewspace partitioning of densely occluded scenes. *Computer Graphics Forum (Proc. Eurographics '98) 17*, 3 (Sept. 1998), 243–254. ISSN 1067-7055.

[COM98] COHEN J., OLANO M., MANOCHA D.: Appearance-preserving simplification. In *SIGGRAPH '98: Proceedings of the 25th annual conference on Computer graphics and interactive techniques* (New York, NY, USA, 1998), ACM, pp. 115–122.

[cor] CORP. N.: Opengl extension registry. http://www.opengl.org/registry.

[Cro77] CROW F. C.: Shadow algorithms for computer graphics. *Computer Graphics (SIGGRAPH '77 Proceedings) 11*, 2 (Summer 1977).

[CT81] COOK R. L., TORRANCE K. E.: A reflectance model for computer graphics. In *SIGGRAPH '81: Proceedings of the 8th annual conference on Computer graphics and interactive techniques* (New York, NY, USA, 1981), ACM, pp. 307–316.

[DBD*07] DRETTAKIS G., BONNEEL N., DACHSBACHER C., LEFEBVRE S., SCHWARZ M., VIAUD-DELMON I.: An interactive perceptual rendering pipeline using

Bibliography

      contrast and spatial masking. In *Rendering Techniques (Proceedings of the Eurographics Symposium on Rendering)* (June 2007), Eurographics.

[DD02]   DUGUET F., DRETTAKIS G.: Robust epsilon visibility. *Computer Graphics (SIGGRAPH'02 Proceedings)* (2002).

[DDSD03] DÉCORET X., DURAND F., SILLION F., DORSEY J.: Billboard clouds for extreme model simplification. In *Proceedings of the ACM Siggraph* (2003), ACM Press.

[DDTP00] DURAND F., DRETTAKIS G., THOLLOT J., PUECH C.: Conservative visibility preprocessing using extended projections. In *SIGGRAPH 2000 Conference Proceedings* (July 2000), Akeley K., (Ed.), Annual Conference Series, ACM SIGGRAPH, Addison Wesley, pp. 239–248.

[Déc05]   DÉCORET X.: N-buffers for efficient depth map query. *Computer Graphics Forum 24*, 3 (2005).

[DL06]   DONNELLY W., LAURITZEN A.: Variance shadow maps. In *I3D '06: Proceedings of the 2006 symposium on Interactive 3D graphics and games* (New York, NY, USA, 2006), ACM, pp. 161–165.

[DN04]   DECAUDIN P., NEYRET F.: Rendering forest scenes in real-time. In *In Proceedings of Eurographics Symposium on Rendering* (2004).

[DS05]   DACHSBACHER C., STAMMINGER M.: Reflective shadow maps. In *Proceedings of the 2005 Symposium on Interactive 3D Graphics, SI3D 2005, April 3-6, 2005, Washington, DC, USA* (2005), pp. 203–231.

[DS06]   DACHSBACHER C., STAMMINGER M.: Splatting indirect illumination. In *Proceedings of the 2006 Symposium on Interactive 3D Graphics, SI3D 2006, March 14-17, 2006, Redwood City, California, USA* (2006), pp. 93–100.

[DSDD07] DACHSBACHER C., STAMMINGER M., DRETTAKIS G., DURAND F.: Implicit visibility and antiradiance for interactive global illumination. *ACM Transaction on Graphics 26*, 3 (2007), 61.

[Dur99]   DURAND F.: *3D Visibility: Analytical Study and Applications.* PhD thesis, Universite Joseph Fourier, Grenoble, France, 1999.

[DWWL05] DAYAL A., WOOLLEY C., WATSON B., LUEBKE D. P.: Adaptive frameless rendering. In *Rendering Techniques* (2005), pp. 265–275.

[ED04]   EISEMANN E., DURAND F.: Flash photography enhancement via intrinsic relighting. In *ACM Transactions on Graphics (Proceedings of Siggraph Conference)* (2004), vol. 23, ACM Press.

Bibliography

[ED07]   EISEMANN E., DÉCORET X.: Visibility sampling on gpu and applications. *Computer Graphics Forum (Proceedings of Eurographics 2007) 26*, 3 (2007).

[EMWVB01] ERIKSON C., MANOCHA D., WILLIAM V. BAXTER I.: Hlods for faster display of large static and dynamic environments. In *I3D '01: Proceedings of the 2001 symposium on Interactive 3D graphics* (New York, NY, USA, 2001), ACM Press, pp. 111–120.

[FC08]   FOX M., COMPTON S.: Ambient occlusive crease shading. *Game Developer Magazine* (March 2008).

[Fer05]   FERNANDO R.: Percentage-closer soft shadows. In *SIGGRAPH '05: ACM SIGGRAPH 2005 Sketches* (New York, NY, USA, 2005), ACM, p. 35.

[FFBG01] FERNANDO R., FERNANDEZ S., BALA K., GREENBERG D. P.: Adaptive shadow maps. In *Computer Graphics (Proceedings of SIGGRAPH '01)* (2001), ACM SIGGRAPH, pp. 387–390.

[FKN80]   FUCHS H., KEDEM Z. M., NAYLOR B. F.: On visible surface generation by a priori tree structures. In *SIGGRAPH '80: Proceedings of the 7th annual conference on Computer graphics and interactive techniques* (New York, NY, USA, 1980), ACM, pp. 124–133.

[FM08]   FILION D., MCNAUGHTON R.: Effects & techniques. In *SIGGRAPH '08: ACM SIGGRAPH 2008 classes* (New York, NY, USA, 2008), ACM, pp. 133–164.

[FS93]   FUNKHOUSER T. A., SÉQUIN C. H.: Adaptive display algorithm for interactive frame rates during visualization of complex virtual environments. In *SIGGRAPH '93: Proceedings of the 20th annual conference on Computer graphics and interactive techniques* (New York, NY, USA, 1993), ACM, pp. 247–254.

[GBK06]   GUTHE M., BALÁZS A., KLEIN R.: Near optimal hierarchical culling: Performance driven use of hardware occlusion queries. In *Eurographics Symposium on Rendering 2006* (June 2006), Akenine-Möller T., Heidrich W., (Eds.), The Eurographics Association.

[GBP06]   GUENNEBAUD G., BARTHE L., PAULIN M.: Real-time soft shadow mapping by backprojection. In *Eurographics Symposium on Rendering (EGSR), Nicosia, Cyprus* (jun 2006), Eurographics, pp. 227–234.

[GBP07]   GUENNEBAUD G., BARTHE L., PAULIN M.: High-Quality Adaptive Soft Shadow Mapping. *Computer Graphics Forum, Eurographics 2007 proceedings 26*, 3 (september 2007), 525–534.

Bibliography

[GGSC96] GORTLER S. J., GRZESZCZUK R., SZELISKI R., COHEN M. F.: The lumigraph. In *SIGGRAPH '96: Proceedings of the 23rd annual conference on Computer graphics and interactive techniques* (New York, NY, USA, 1996), ACM, pp. 43–54.

[GJW08] GUERRERO P., JESCHKE S., WIMMER M.: Real-time indirect illumination and soft shadows in dynamic scenes using spherical lights. *Computer Graphics Forum 27*, 8 (Oct. 2008), 2154–2168.

[Gla84] GLASSNER A.: Space subdivision for fast ray tracing. *CGA 4*, 10 (1984), 15–22.

[GM90] GIGUS Z., MALIK J.: Computing the aspect graph for line drawings of polyhedral objects. *IEEE Transactions on Pattern Analysis and Machine Intelligence 12*, 2 (Feb. 1990), 113–122.

[GM05] GOBBETTI E., MARTON F.: Far Voxels – a multiresolution framework for interactive rendering of huge complex 3d models on commodity graphics platforms. *ACM Transactions on Graphics 24*, 3 (August 2005), 878–885. Proc. SIGGRAPH 2005.

[Gre94] GREENE N.: Detecting intersection of a rectangular solid and a convex polyhedron. In *Graphics Gems IV*. Academic Press, Boston, 1994, pp. 74–82.

[GS87] GOLDSMITH J., SALMON J.: Automatic creation of object hierarchies for ray tracing. *IEEE Comput. Graph. Appl. 7*, 5 (1987), 14–20.

[GSF99] GOTSMAN C., SUDARSKY O., FAYMAN J. A.: Optimized occlusion culling using five-dimensional subdivision. *Computers and Graphics 23*, 5 (Oct. 1999), 645–654.

[GSYM03] GOVINDARAJU N. K., SUD A., YOON S.-E., MANOCHA D.: Interactive visibility culling in complex environments using occlusion-switches. In *SI3D* (2003), pp. 103–112.

[GTGB84] GORAL C. M., TORRANCE K. E., GREENBERG D. P., BATTAILE B.: Modeling the interaction of light between diffuse surfaces. *SIGGRAPH Comput. Graph. 18*, 3 (1984), 213–222.

[GW07] GIEGL M., WIMMER M.: Unpopping: Solving the image-space blend problem for smooth discrete lod transitions. *Computer Graphics Forum 26*, 1 (Mar. 2007), 46–49.

[HAM02] HAINES E., AKENINE-MOLLER T.: *Real-Time Rendering (2nd Edition)*. AK Peters, Ltd., July 2002.

Bibliography

[Hav00]   HAVRAN V.: *Heuristic Ray Shooting Algorithms*. Ph.d. thesis, Department of Computer Science and Engineering, Faculty of Electrical Engineering, Czech Technical University in Prague, November 2000.

[HBS03]   HAVRAN V., BITTNER J., SEIDEL H.-P.: Exploiting temporal coherence in ray casted walkthroughs. In *SCCG '03: Proceedings of the 19th spring conference on Computer graphics* (New York, NY, USA, 2003), ACM, pp. 149–155.

[HDS03]   HAUMONT D., DEBEIR O., SILLION F.: Volumetric cell-and-portal generation. *Computer Graphics Forum 22*, 3 (September 2003), 303–312.

[HLHS03]   HASENFRATZ J.-M., LAPIERRE M., HOLZSCHUCH N., SILLION F. X.: A survey of real-time soft shadows algorithms. *Comput. Graph. Forum 22*, 4 (2003), 753–774.

[HMN05]   HAUMONT D., MÄKINEN O., NIRENSTEIN S.: A low dimensional framework for exact polygon-to-polygon occlusion queries. In *Proc. Eurographics Symposium on Rendering* (June 2005), pp. 211–222.

[HMS06]   HUNT W., MARK W. R., STOLL G.: Fast kd-tree construction with an adaptive error-bounded heuristic. In *2006 IEEE Symposium on Interactive Ray Tracing* (Sept. 2006), IEEE.

[Hop96]   HOPPE H.: Progressive meshes. In *SIGGRAPH '96: Proceedings of the 23rd annual conference on Computer graphics and interactive techniques* (New York, NY, USA, 1996), ACM, pp. 99–108.

[HSLM02]   HILLESLAND K., SALOMON B., LASTRA A., MANOCHA D.: *Fast and Simple Occlusion Culling Using Hardware-Based Depth Queries*. Tech. Rep. TR02-039, Department of Computer Science, University of North Carolina - Chapel Hill, Sept. 12 2002.

[Jes05]   JESCHKE S.: *Accelerating the Rendering Process Using Impostors*. PhD thesis, Institute of Computer Graphics and Algorithms, Vienna University of Technology, Favoritenstrasse 9-11/186, A-1040 Vienna, Austria, Mar. 2005.

[JMW07]   JESCHKE S., MANTLER S., WIMMER M.: Interactive smooth and curved shell mapping. In *Rendering Techniques 2007 (Proceedings Eurographics Symposium on Rendering)* (6 2007), Kautz J., Pattanaik S., (Eds.), Eurographics, Eurographics Association, pp. 351–360.

[Jun06]   JUNKER G.: *Pro OGRE 3D Programming*, 1 ed. Apress, September 2006.

[JWS02]   JESCHKE S., WIMMER M., SCHUMAN H.: Layered Environment-Map Impostors for Arbitrary Scenes. In *Proc. Graphics Interface* (May 2002), pp. 1–8.

Bibliography

[KA06] KONTKANEN J., AILA T.: Ambient occlusion for animated characters. In *Rendering Techniques 2006 (Eurographics Symposium on Rendering)* (jun 2006), Wolfgang Heidrich T. A.-M., (Ed.), Eurographics.

[KA07] KIRK A. G., ARIKAN O.: Real-time ambient occlusion for dynamic character skins. In *I3D '07: Proceedings of the 2007 symposium on Interactive 3D graphics and games* (New York, NY, USA, 2007), ACM, pp. 47–52.

[Kaj86] KAJIYA J. T.: The rendering equation. *SIGGRAPH Comput. Graph. 20*, 4 (1986), 143–150.

[KCCO01] KOLTUN V., CHRYSANTHOU Y., COHEN-OR C.-O.: Hardware-Accelerated from-Region visibility using a dual ray space. In *Rendering Techniques '01 (Proceedings of the Eurographics Workshop on Rendering 01)* (2001), pp. 205–216.

[Kel97] KELLER A.: Instant radiosity. In *Proceedings of SIGGRAPH 97* (Aug. 1997), Computer Graphics Proceedings, Annual Conference Series, pp. 49–56.

[KH01] KELLER A., HEIDRICH W.: Interleaved sampling. In *Proceedings of the 12th Eurographics Workshop on Rendering Techniques* (London, UK, 2001), Springer-Verlag, pp. 269–276.

[KHM*98] KLOSOWSKI J. T., HELD M., MITCHELL J. S. B., SOWIZRAL H., ZIKAN K.: Efficient collision detection using bounding volume hierarchies of k-dops. *IEEE Transactions on Visualization and Computer Graphics 4*, 1 (1998), 21–36.

[KL05] KONTKANEN J., LAINE S.: Ambient occlusion fields. In *I3D '05: Proceedings of the 2005 symposium on Interactive 3D graphics and games* (New York, NY, USA, 2005), ACM, pp. 41–48.

[Kne09] KNECHT M.: *Real-Time Global Illumination Using Temporal Coherence*. Master's thesis, Institute of Computer Graphics and Algorithms, Vienna University of Technology, Favoritenstrasse 9-11/186, A-1040 Vienna, Austria, July 2009.

[KS00] KLOSOWSKI J. T., SILVA C. T.: The prioritized-layered projection algorithm for visible set estimation. In *IEEE Transactions on Visualization and Computer Graphics*, Hagen H., Ebert D. S., (Eds.), vol. 6 (2). IEEE Computer Society, 2000, pp. 108–123.

[KS01] KLOSOWSKI J. T., SILVA. C. T.: Efficient conservative visibility culling using the prioritized-layered projection algorithm. *IEEE Transactions on Visualization and Computer Graphics 7*, 4 (Oct. 2001), 365–379.

Bibliography

[KS05]   KOVALCIK V., SOCHOR J.: Occlusion culling with statistically optimized occlusion queries. In *WSCG (Short Papers)* (2005), pp. 109–112.

[KS06]   KORTENJAN M., SCHOMAKER G.: Size equivalent cluster trees (sec-trees) realtime rendering of large industrial scenes. In *Afrigaph '06: Proceedings of the 4th international conference on Computer graphics, virtual reality, visualisation and interaction in Africa* (New York, NY, USA, 2006), ACM Press, pp. 107–116.

[KTI*01] KANEKO T., TAKAHEI T., INAMI M., KAWAKAMI N., YANAGIDA Y., MAEDA T., TACHI S.: Detailed shape representation with parallax mapping. In *In Proceedings of the ICAT 2001* (2001), pp. 205–208.

[Lai05] LAINE S.: A general algorithm for output-sensitive visibility preprocessing. In *Proceedings of ACM SIGGRAPH 2005 Symposium on Interactive 3D Graphics and Games* (2005), ACM Press, pp. 31–39.

[Lan02] LANDIS H.: Production-ready global illumination. In *Proceedings of the conference on SIGGRAPH 2002 course notes 16* (2002).

[LCOC03] LERNER A., COHEN-OR D., CHRYSANTHOU Y.: Breaking the walls: Scene partitioning and portal creation. In *Pacific Graphics* (2003).

[Leh07] LEHTINEN J.: A framework for precomputed and captured light transport. *ACM Trans. Graph. 26*, 4 (2007), 13.

[LG95a] LUEBKE D., GEORGES C.: Portals and mirrors: Simple, fast evaluation of potentially visible sets. In *1995 Symposium on Interactive 3D Graphics* (Apr. 1995), ACM SIGGRAPH, pp. 105–106.

[LG95b] LUEBKE D., GEORGES C.: Portals and mirrors: Simple, fast evaluation of potentially visible sets. In *1995 Symposium on Interactive 3D Graphics* (Apr. 1995), Hanrahan P., Winget J., (Eds.), ACM SIGGRAPH, pp. 105–106.

[LGQ*08] LLOYD B., GOVINDARAJU N. K., QUAMMEN C., MOLNAR S. E., MANOCHA D.: Logarithmic perspective shadow maps. *ACM Trans. Graph. 27*, 4 (2008).

[LH96a] LEVOY M., HANRAHAN P.: Light field rendering. In *SIGGRAPH* (1996), pp. 31–42.

[LH96b] LEVOY M., HANRAHAN P.: Light field rendering. In *SIGGRAPH 96 Conference Proceedings* (Aug. 1996), Rushmeier H., (Ed.), Annual Conference Series, ACM SIGGRAPH, Addison Wesley, pp. 31–42. held in New Orleans, Louisiana, 04-09 August 1996.

Bibliography

[LMD05] LIM S.-N., MITTAL A., DAVIS L.: Constructing task visibility intervals for a surveillance system. In *VSSN '05: Proceedings of the third ACM international workshop on Video surveillance & sensor networks* (New York, NY, USA, 2005), ACM, pp. 141–148.

[LSCO03] LEYVAND T., SORKINE O., COHEN-OR D.: Ray space factorization for from-region visibility. *ACM Transactions on Graphics (TOG) 22*, 3 (2003), 595–604.

[LSK*07] LAINE S., SARANSAARI H., KONTKANEN J., LEHTINEN J., AILA T.: Incremental instant radiosity for real-time indirect illumination. In *Proceedings of Eurographics Symposium on Rendering 2007* (2007), Eurographics Association, pp. 277–286.

[LSLS09] LAINE S., SILTANEN S., LOKKI T., SAVIOJA L.: Accelerated beam tracing algorithm. *Applied Acoustics 70*, 1 (2009), 172–181.

[MAM05] MORA F., AVENEAU L., MÉRIAUX M.: Coherent and exact polygon-to-polygon visibility. In *Proceedings of the International Conference in Central Europe on Computer Graphics, Visualization and Computer Vision* (Janvier 2005).

[Max88] MAX N. L.: Horizon mapping: shadows for bump-mapped surfaces. *The Visual Computer 4*, 2 (1988), 109–117.

[MB90] MACDONALD J. D., BOOTH K. S.: Heuristics for ray tracing using space subdivision. *Visual Computer 6*, 6 (1990), 153–65. criteria for building octree (actually BSP) efficiency structures.

[MBM*01] MEISSNER M., BARTZ D., MUELLER G., HUETTNER T., EINIGHAMMER J.: Generation of decomposition hierarchies for efficient occlusion culling of large polygonal models. In *Proceedings of the Vision Modeling and Visualization Conference 2001* (Nov. 21–23 2001), pp. 225–232.

[MBMD98] MENEVEAUX D., BOUATOUCH K., MAISEL E., DELMONT R.: A new partitioning method for architectural environments. *Journal of Visualization and Computer Animation 9*, 4 (1998), 195–213.

[MBW06] MATTAUSCH O., BITTNER J., WIMMER M.: Adaptive visibility-driven view cell construction. In *Rendering Techniques 2006 (Proceedings of Eurographics Symposium on Rendering)* (June 2006), Heidrich W., Akenine-Moller T., (Eds.), Eurographics, Eurographics Association, pp. 195–206.

[MBW08] MATTAUSCH O., BITTNER J., WIMMER M.: Chc++: Coherent hierarchical culling revisited. *Computer Graphics Forum (Proceedings of Eurographics 2008) 27*, 3 (Apr. 2008), 221–230.

Bibliography

[MBWW07] MATTAUSCH O., BITTNER J., WONKA P., WIMMER M.: Optimized subdivisions for preprocessed visibility. In *Proceedings of Graphics Interface 2007* (May 2007), pp. 335–342.

[MCTH05] MURRIETA-CID R., TOVAR B., HUTCHINSON S.: A sampling-based motion planning approach to maintain visibility of unpredictable targets. *Auton. Robots 19*, 3 (2005), 285–300.

[MHMT05] MANTLER S., HESINA G., MAIERHOFER S., TOBLER F. R.: Real-time rendering of vegetation and trees in urban environments. *in Proceedings of CORP -International Symposium on Information and Communication Technologies in Urban and Spatial planning* (2005), pp. 227–230.

[Mit07] MITTRING M.: Finding next gen - cryengine 2. In *Proceedings of the conference on SIGGRAPH 2007 course notes, course 28, Advanced Real-Time Rendering in 3D Graphics and Games* (2007), ACM Press, pp. 97–121.

[MMAH07] MALMER M., MALMER F., ASSARSSON U., HOLZSCHUCH N.: Fast precomputed ambient occlusion for proximity shadows. *journal of graphics tools 12*, 2 (2007), 59–71.

[MSW10] MATTAUSCH O., SCHERZER D., WIMMER M.: High-quality screen-space ambient occlusion using temporal coherence. *Computer Graphics Forum (to appear)* (2010),

[MT90] MARTELLO S., TOTH P.: *Knapsack Problems: Algorithms and Computer Implementations*. John Wiley & Sons Inc., New York, 1990.

[MT97] MÖLLER T., TRUMBORE B.: Fast, minimum storage ray-triangle intersection. *Journal of graphics, gpu, and game tools 2*, 1 (1997), 21–28.

[MTF03] MANTLER S., TOBLER R. F., FUHRMANN A. L.: *The State of the Art in Realtime Rendering of Vegetation*. Tech. rep., VRVis Research Center for Virtual Reality and Visualization, Vienna, Austria, 2003.

[NB04a] NIRENSTEIN S., BLAKE E.: Hardware accelerated aggressive visibility preprocessing using adaptive sampling. In *Rendering Technqiues 2004* (2004), pp. 207–216.

[NB04b] NIRENSTEIN S., BLAKE E.: Hardware accelerated visibility preprocessing using adaptive sampling. In *Rendering Techniques 2004* (2004), pp. 207–216.

[NBG02] NIRENSTEIN S., BLAKE E., GAIN J.: Exact from-region visibility culling. In *Rendering Techniques 2002* (2002), pp. 191–202.

Bibliography

[NRH03] NG R., RAMAMOORTHI R., HANRAHAN P.: All-frequency shadows using non-linear wavelet lighting approximation. *ACM Trans. Graph. 22*, 3 (2003), 376–381.

[NSL99] NISSOUX C., SIMEON T., LAUMOND J.: Visibility based probabilistic roadmaps. In *Proceedings of the IEEE International Conference on Intelligent Robots and Systems* (1999), pp. 1316–1321.

[NSL*07] NEHAB D., SANDER P. V., LAWRENCE J., TATARCHUK N., ISIDORO J. R.: Accelerating real-time shading with reverse reprojection caching. In *Proceedings of the 22nd ACM SIGGRAPH/EUROGRAPHICS symposium on Graphics Hardware 2007* (Aire-la-Ville, Switzerland, Switzerland, 2007), Eurographics Association, pp. 25–35.

[PD90] PLANTINGA H., DYER C.: Visibility, occlusion, and the aspect graph. *International Journal of Computer Vision 5*, 2 (1990), 137–160.

[PG04] PHARR M., GREEN S.: *Ambient Occlusion*. Addison-Wesley Professional, 2004, ch. 14, pp. 279–292.

[Pit99] PITO R.: A solution to the next best view problem for automated surface acquisition. *IEEE Trans. Pattern Anal. Mach. Intell. 21*, 10 (1999), 1016–1030.

[PO06] POLICARPO F., OLIVEIRA M. M.: Relief mapping of non-height-field surface details. In *I3D '06: Proceedings of the 2006 symposium on Interactive 3D graphics and games* (New York, NY, USA, 2006), ACM, pp. 55–62.

[PSALY*08] PITCHAYA SITTHI-AMORN P., LAWRENCE J., YANG L., SANDER P. V., NEHAB D.: An improved shading cache for modern gpus. In *GH '08: Proceedings of the 23rd ACM SIGGRAPH/EUROGRAPHICS symposium on Graphics hardware* (Aire-la-Ville, Switzerland, Switzerland, 2008), Eurographics Association, pp. 95–101.

[RGK*08] RITSCHEL T., GROSCH T., KIM M. H., SEIDEL H.-P., DACHSBACHER C., KAUTZ J.: Imperfect shadow maps for efficient computation of indirect illumination. *ACM Transactions on Graphics (Proc. SIGGRAPH ASIA 2008) 27*, 5 (2008), 129.

[RGS09] RITSCHEL T., GROSCH T., SEIDEL H.-P.: Approximating dynamic global illumination in image space. In *I3D '09: Proceedings of the 2009 symposium on Interactive 3D graphics and games* (New York, NY, USA, 2009), ACM, pp. 75–82.

[RH94] ROHLF J., HELMAN J.: Iris performer: a high performance multiprocessing toolkit for real-time 3d graphics. In *SIGGRAPH '94: Proceedings of the 21st*

Bibliography

annual conference on Computer graphics and interactive techniques (New York, NY, USA, 1994), ACM, pp. 381–394.

[Ros07] ROSADO G.: Motion Blur as a Post-Processing Effect. Addison-Wesley Professional, 2007, ch. 27, pp. 575–576.

[RSC87] REEVES W. T., SALESIN D. H., COOK R. L.: Rendering antialiased shadows with depth maps. SIGGRAPH Comput. Graph. 21, 4 (1987), 283–291.

[RSH05] RESHETOV A., SOUPIKOV A., HURLEY J.: Multi-level ray tracing algorithm. In SIGGRAPH '05: ACM SIGGRAPH 2005 Papers (New York, NY, USA, 2005), ACM Press, pp. 1176–1185.

[RWS*06] REN Z., WANG R., SNYDER J., ZHOU K., LIU X., SUN B., SLOAN P.-P., BAO H., PENG Q., GUO B.: Real-time soft shadows in dynamic scenes using spherical harmonic exponentiation. In SIGGRAPH '06: ACM SIGGRAPH 2006 Papers (New York, NY, USA, 2006), ACM, pp. 977–986.

[SA07] SHANMUGAM P., ARIKAN O.: Hardware accelerated ambient occlusion techniques on gpus. In Symbosium of Interactive 3D graphics and games (2007), pp. 73–80.

[SALY*08] SITTHI-AMORN P., LAWRENCE J., YANG L., SANDER P. V., NEHAB D., XI J.: Automated reprojection-based pixel shader optimization. ACM Transactions on Graphics (Proc. of SIGGRAPH Asia 2008 27, 5 (2008), 127.

[SBS04] STANEKER D., BARTZ D., STRASSER W.: Occlusion culling in OpenSG PLUS. Computers and Graphics 28, 1 (Feb. 2004), 87–92.

[SDDS00] SCHAUFLER G., DORSEY J., DÉCORET X., SILLION F.: Conservative volumetric visibility with occluder fusion. In Computer Graphics (SIGGRAPH 2000 Proceedings) (2000), pp. 229–238.

[SGHS98] SHADE J., GORTLER S., HE L.-W., SZELISKI R.: Layered depth images. In SIGGRAPH '98: Proceedings of the 25th annual conference on Computer graphics and interactive techniques (New York, NY, USA, 1998), ACM, pp. 231–242.

[SGNS07] SLOAN P.-P. J., GOVINDARAJU N. K., NOWROUZEZAHRAI D., SNYDER J.: Image-based proxy accumulation for real-time soft global illumination. In Pacific Conference on Computer Graphics and Applications (2007), pp. 97–105.

Bibliography

[SGS*04]   SALOMON B., GOVINDARAJU N. K., SUD A., GAYLE R., LIN M. C., MANOCHA D.: Accelerating line of sight computation using graphics processing units. In *Proceedings. of Army Science Conference* (2004).

[SGwHS98] SHADE J., GORTLER S., WEI HE L., SZELISKI R.: Layered depth images. In *Proc. ACM SIGGRAPH 98* (1998), pp. 231–242.

[Shi05]   SHISHKOVTSOV O.: *Deferred Shading in S.T.A.L.K.E.R.* Addison-Wesley Professional, 2005, ch. 2, pp. 143–166.

[SIMP06]   SEGOVIA B., IEHL J.-C., MITANCHEY R., PÉROCHE B.: Non-interleaved deferred shading of interleaved sample patterns. In *Proceedings of the 22nd ACM SIGGRAPH/EUROGRAPHICS symposium on Graphics Hardware 2006* (2006), pp. 53–60.

[SIP06]   SEGOVIA B., IEHL J.-C., PÉROCHE B.: Bidirectional Instant Radiosity. In *Proceedings of the 17th Eurographics Workshop on Rendering* (June 2006).

[SIP07]   SEGOVIA B., IEHL J. C., PÉROCHE B.: Metropolis instant radiosity. *Computer Graphics Forum 26*, 3 (2007), 425–434.

[SJW07]   SCHERZER D., JESCHKE S., WIMMER M.: Pixel-correct shadow maps with temporal reprojection and shadow test confidence. In *Rendering Techniques 2007 (Proceedings Eurographics Symposium on Rendering)* (June 2007), Kautz J., Pattanaik S., (Eds.), Eurographics, Eurographics Association, pp. 45–50.

[SKS02]   SLOAN P.-P., KAUTZ J., SNYDER J.: Precomputed radiance transfer for real-time rendering in dynamic, low-frequency lighting environments. In *SIGGRAPH '02: Proceedings of the 29th annual conference on Computer graphics and interactive techniques* (New York, NY, USA, 2002), ACM, pp. 527–536.

[SLCO*04] SAYER E., LERNER A., COHEN-OR D., CHRYSANTHOU Y., DEUSSEN O.: Aggressive visibility for rendering extremely complex foliage scenes. In *Proceedings of the Korea-Israel Bi-National Conference* (2004).

[SLS*96]   SHADE J., LISCHINSKI D., SALESIN D. H., DEROSE T., SNYDER J.: Hierarchical image caching for accelerated walkthroughs of complex environments. In *SIGGRAPH '96: Proceedings of the 23rd annual conference on Computer graphics and interactive techniques* (New York, NY, USA, 1996), ACM, pp. 75–82.

[SPNP96]   SBERT M., PUEYO X., NEUMANN L., PURGATHOFER W.: Global multipath monte carlo algorithms for radiosity. *The Visual Computer 12*, 2 (1996), 47–61.

Bibliography

[SS96] SCHAUFLER G., STÜRZLINGER W.: A three dimensional image cache for virtual reality. *Comput. Graph. Forum 15*, 3 (1996), 227–236.

[SS07] SCHWARZ M., STAMMINGER M.: Bitmask soft shadows. *Comput. Graph. Forum 26*, 3 (2007), 515–524.

[SSMW09] SCHERZER D., SCHWÄRZLER M., MATTAUSCH O., WIMMER M.: Real-time soft shadows using temporal coherence. In *Advances in Visual Computing: 5th International Symposium on Visual Computing (ISVC 2009)* (Dec. 2009), Bebis G., Boyle R., Parvin B., Koracin D., Kuno Y., Wang J., Pajarola R., Lindstrom P., Hinkenjann A., Encarnacao M., Silva C., Coming D., (Eds.), Lecture Notes in Computer Science, Springer, pp.

[ST90] SAITO T., TAKAHASHI T.: Comprehensible rendering of 3-d shapes. *SIGGRAPH Computer Graphics 24*, 4 (1990), 197–206.

[Stu99] STUERZLINGER W.: Imaging all visible surfaces. In *Proc. Graphics Interface 1999* (June 1999), pp. 115–122.

[SVNB99] SAONA-VÁZQUEZ C., NAVAZO I., BRUNET P.: The visibility octree: a data structure for 3D navigation. *Computers and Graphics 23*, 5 (Oct. 1999), 635–643.

[SW08] SCHERZER D., WIMMER M.: Frame sequential interpolation for discrete level-of-detail rendering. *Computer Graphics Forum (Proceedings EGSR 2008) 27*, 4 (June 2008), 1175–1181.

[SW09] SMEDBERG N., WRIGHT D.: Rendering techniques in gears of war 2, 2009.

[Tel92a] TELLER S. J.: Computing the antipenumbra of an area light source. In *Computer Graphics (Proceedings of SIGGRAPH '92)* (July 1992), pp. 139–148.

[Tel92b] TELLER S. J.: *Visibility Computations in Densely Occluded Polyhedral Environments*. PhD thesis, Dept. of Computer Science, University of California, Berkeley, 1992. Also available as Technical Report UCB//CSD-92-708.

[TMD*04] TAWARA T., MYSZKOWSKI K., DMITRIEV K., HAVRAN V., DAMEZ C., SEIDEL H.-P.: Exploiting temporal coherence in global illumination. In *SCCG '04: Proceedings of the 20th spring conference on Computer graphics* (New York, NY, USA, 2004), ACM, pp. 23–33.

[TS91] TELLER S. J., SÉQUIN C. H.: Visibility preprocessing for interactive walk-throughs. In *Proceedings of SIGGRAPH '91* (July 1991), pp. 61–69.

[vdPS99] VAN DE PANNE M., STEWART A. J.: Effective compression techniques for precomputed visibility. In *Rendering Techniques* (1999), pp. 305–316.

Bibliography

[VMH*05] VERDESCA M., MUNRO J., HOFFMAN M., BAUER M., MANOCHA D.: Using graphics processing units to accelerate onesaf: A case study in technology transition. In *Journal of Defense Modeling and Simulation* (2005).

[Wal07] WALD I.: On fast construction of sah-based bounding volume hierarchies. *Symposium on Interactive Ray Tracing 0* (2007), 33–40.

[WH00] WANG X., HICKERNELL F. J.: Randomized halton sequences. *Mathematical and Computer Modelling 32* (2000), 2000.

[WIK*06] WALD I., IZE T., KENSLER A., KNOLL A., PARKER S. G.: Ray Tracing Animated Scenes using Coherent Grid Traversal. *ACM Transactions on Graphics* (2006), 485–493. (Proceedings of ACM SIGGRAPH 2006).

[Wil78] WILLIAMS L.: Casting curved shadows on curved surfaces. In *Computer Graphics (SIGGRAPH '78 Proceedings)* (Aug. 1978), pp. 270–274.

[Wim01] WIMMER M.: *Representing and Rendering Distant Objects for Real-Time Visualization*. PhD thesis, Institute of Computer Graphics and Algorithms, Vienna University of Technology, Favoritenstrasse 9-11/186, A-1040 Vienna, Austria, June 2001.

[WM03] WILSON A., MANOCHA D.: Simplifying complex environments using incremental textured depth meshes. *ACM Trans. Graph. 22*, 3 (2003), 678–688.

[WMS06] WOOP S., MARMITT G., SLUSALLEK P.: B-KD Trees for Hardware Accelerated Ray Tracing of Dynamic Scenes. In *Proceedings of Graphics Hardware* (2006), pp. 67–77.

[Won01] WONKA P.: *Occlusion Culling for Real-Time Rendering of Urban Environments*. PhD thesis, Institute of Computer Graphics, Vienna University of Technology, 2001.

[WSP04] WIMMER M., SCHERZER D., PURGATHOFER W.: Light space perspective shadow maps. In *Rendering Techniques 2004 (Proceedings Eurographics Symposium on Rendering)* (June 2004), Keller A., Jensen H. W., (Eds.), Eurographics, Eurographics Association, pp. 143–151.

[WW03] WIMMER M., WONKA P.: Rendering time estimation for real-time rendering. In *Rendering Techniques* (2003), pp. 118–129.

[WWS00] WONKA P., WIMMER M., SCHMALSTIEG D.: Visibility preprocessing with occluder fusion for urban walkthroughs. In *Rendering Techniques 2000* (June 2000), pp. 71–82.

[WWZ*06] WONKA P., WIMMER M., ZHOU K., MAIERHOFER S., HESINA G., RESHETOV A.: Guided visibility sampling. *ACM Transactions on Graphics 25*, 3 (July 2006), 494–502. Proceedings ACM SIGGRAPH 2006.

Bibliography

[YNS*09] YANG L., NEHAB D., SANDER P. V., SITTHI-AMORN P., LAWRENCE J., HOPPE H.: Amortized supersampling. *ACM Transactions on Graphics (Proc. of SIGGRAPH Asia 2009) 28*, 5 (2009), 135.

[ZHL*05] ZHOU K., HU Y., LIN S., GUO B., SHUM H.-Y.: Precomputed shadow fields for dynamic scenes. *ACM Transactions on Graphics 24*, 3 (Aug. 2005), 1196–1201.

[ZIK98] ZHUKOV S., IONES A., KRONIN G.: An ambient light illumination model. In *Rendering Techniques* (1998), pp. 45–56.

[ZMHH97] ZHANG H., MANOCHA D., HUDSON T., HOFF III K. E.: Visibility culling using hierarchical occlusion maps. In *SIGGRAPH 97 Conference Proceedings* (Aug. 1997), Whitted T., (Ed.), Annual Conference Series, ACM SIGGRAPH, Addison Wesley, pp. 77–88. ISBN 0-89791-896-7.

[ZSXL06] ZHANG F., SUN H., XU L., LUN L. K.: Parallel-split shadow maps for large-scale virtual environments. In *VRCIA '06: Proceedings of the 2006 ACM international conference on Virtual reality continuum and its applications* (New York, NY, USA, 2006), ACM Press, pp. 311–318.

Die VDM Verlagsservicegesellschaft sucht für wissenschaftliche Verlage abgeschlossene und herausragende

Dissertationen, Habilitationen, Diplomarbeiten, Master Theses, Magisterarbeiten usw.

für die kostenlose Publikation als Fachbuch.

Sie verfügen über eine Arbeit, die hohen inhaltlichen und formalen Ansprüchen genügt, und haben Interesse an einer honorarvergüteten Publikation?

Dann senden Sie bitte erste Informationen über sich und Ihre Arbeit per Email an *info@vdm-vsg.de*.

Sie erhalten kurzfristig unser Feedback!

VDM Verlagsservicegesellschaft mbH
Dudweiler Landstr. 99   Telefon +49 681 3720 174
D - 66123 Saarbrücken   Fax   +49 681 3720 1749

www.vdm-vsg.de

Die VDM Verlagsservicegesellschaft mbH vertritt

Printed by Books on Demand GmbH, Norderstedt / Germany